James R. Milne

**Considerations on Eucharistic Worship**

True and false doctrine of the Eucharistic Sacrifice

James R. Milne

**Considerations on Eucharistic Worship**
*True and false doctrine of the Eucharistic Sacrifice*

ISBN/EAN: 9783337285753

Printed in Europe, USA, Canada, Australia, Japan

Cover: Foto ©Lupo / pixelio.de

More available books at **www.hansebooks.com**

# Considerations
## on
# Eucharistic Worship.

# Considerations on Eucharistic Worship,

OR,

TRUE AND FALSE DOCTRINE OF THE EUCHARISTIC SACRIFICE.

BY THE REV.

J. R. MILNE, M.A.,

VICAR OF ROUGHAM, NORFOLK.

London:
SKEFFINGTON & SON, PICCADILLY, W.

—

1893.

# Advertisement.

THE writer desires to commend these considerations on Eucharistic worship, and the criticism of Roman doctrine contained in them, to the attention more especially of those Anglican High Churchmen of the modern so-called Catholic school, who, because they feel keenly the deficiencies, spiritual and liturgical, of ordinary Anglican worship, are too apt to accept, without sufficient examination, the Roman theory and practice of the Mass as a standard of Catholic orthodoxy and an ideal form of true Christian worship. It is assumed by many members of this school that it is only the Church of England that has "suffered grievously from degenerate and heretical tendencies within her borders," which have silenced "the voice of Catholic orthodoxy" and suppressed "the witness of Catholic ritual." But the endeavour is here made to shew that the voice of Catholic orthodoxy, even on the question of the Eucharist, is not to be heard in the Church of Rome, and that Roman practice and ritual has suppressed the witness which the Canon of the Mass itself bears to the truer, more original form and practice of Eucharistic worship. Whatever degenerate and heretical tendencies there may be in Anglicanism and Protestantism are referable to, and are the direct results of similar tendencies in Romanism. It will not do for Anglicans to assume that Protestantism alone is heretical and Romanism not, or that our quarrel with Rome is merely about Papal infallibility and Anglican Orders, and a few other trifling points of practice only. Romanism is very far from being synonymous with Catholic orthodoxy, and even Protestantism may justly claim to bear a true witness to some important points of Catholic orthodoxy which Romanism denies.

In another work, not yet published, the writer has endeavoured to subject to a most careful dogmatic examination the various contradictory theories of Roman theologians with regard to the nature of the Eucharistic sacrifice, the character of which manifests the prevalence of as "degenerate and heretical tendencies" in Romanism as any in Protestantism, and the very existence of which sufficiently attests the fact that the Roman Church has never possessed since earlier mediæval times a true doctrine on the subject, and that her later practice relative thereto has rested on an altogether unsound foundation, as it has also been at variance with older, more venerable, liturgical tradition.

# Contents.

|  | PAGE |
|---|---|
| SCANDAL of Protestant neglect and depreciation of Eucharistic service | 1 |
| The Eucharist the true sacrifice of Christian faith and worship | 2 |
| Its observance the practical confession of faith in the revealed mysteries of the Trinity and the Incarnation | 2 |
| Its observance, the true confession of faith in Christ's Atonement.. | 3 |
| The duty of its objective observance apart from the subjective observance of individual communion.. | 5 |
| Scandal of Roman doctrine and practice of the Mass | 7 |
| Incidental discussion of Tridentine doctrine of justification.. | 9 |
| Tridentine doctrine of Christ's exercise of Melchizedek Priesthood.. | 12 |
| Misapplication of the teaching of Epistle to the Hebrews | 14 |
| Double falsehood in Tridentine doctrine of Christ's exercise of Melchizedek priesthood in the first Eucharist | 17 |
| In the Eucharistic institution Christ began the offering of His sacrifice of the Cross, offered no new sacrifice | 21 |
| What is the meaning of "Do this"? | 22 |
| What is the true "Melchizedek-offering" of Christ? | 25 |
| Discrepancy between teaching of Aquinas and Council of Trent | 26 |

|  | PAGE |
|---|---|
| Confusion of the Sacrifice of the Church with the Sacrifice of Christ | 29 |
| Meaning of "unbloody offering" as applied to the Eucharist | 30 |
| Ambiguity of Tridentine assertion of identity of sacrificial victim | 32 |
| Christ offers no new offering of self-humiliation | 35 |
| The Church's Eucharistic offering of bread and wine, the condition of her participation in the heavenly offering of Christ | 37 |
| No difference in Christ's mode of offering | 38 |
| The Tridentine assertion of "true and proper sacrifice" | 39 |
| The Tridentine teaching opposed to that of S. Thomas on this point | 41 |
| Imperfect conception of the sacrifice of the Cross | 42 |
| The propitiatory character of the Mass | 43 |
| Jesuit speculations on the nature of the "true and proper sacrifice" in the Mass | 43 |
| The witness which these speculations bear against Tridentine doctrine | 45 |
| Later Roman views of Christ's heavenly offering—Döllinger | 47 |
| Criticism of the view of the earthly offering as a reproduction of the heavenly | 47 |
| Thalhofer's idea of the heavenly offering and the Eucharistic in connection therewith | 50 |
| Scheeben's right idea of the Eucharistic offering as the means of making present the heavenly | 51 |

|  | PAGE |
|---|---|
| But his wrong idea of the Eucharistic offering as consisting in Transubstantiation | 53 |
| No double sacrifice of Christ's Body and Blood | 54 |
| The doctrine of Transubstantiation incompatible with the doctrine of the heavenly offering | 55 |
| Roman doctrine inconsistent with the Canon of the Mass | 57 |
| Roman practice inconsistent with the Canon | 59 |
| The Canon not the private prayer of the priest, but the public prayer of the Church | 61 |
| The secret recitation of the Canon has given rise to false ideas of the Eucharistic consecration and Eucharistic worship | 62 |
| The Canon testifies that full consecration is not effected by the mere utterance of the words of Institution | 63 |
| The Roman idea of Transubstantiation falsifies the true idea of Communion | 65 |
| Doctrine of "the unworthy partaking" considered | 66 |
| The true Transubstantiation is only in worthy communion | 68 |
| The suppression of the Canon has injuriously affected the whole idea of Eucharistic worship | 69 |
| Romanism has introduced a false subjectivism into the worship of God, and a false objectivism in the worship of Saints | 70 |
| It supersedes the worship of the heavenly Christ by the worship of a sacramental Christ | 72 |
| Significance of the liturgical invocation of the Holy Ghost | 73 |
| The true objective worship of Christ as our heavenly High Priest | 74 |

| | PAGE |
|---|---|
| The Roman idea of Eucharistic worship has injuriously affected the whole structure of the Eucharistic service | 77 |
| The substitution of individual subjective devotion for true public prayer and intercession | 79 |
| Significance of the Eucharistic lections | 79 |
| In what respect is the worship of the Church the continuation of the worship of the Synagogue and of the Temple | 80 |
| The cause of the curtailment of Eucharistic Psalms and lections in the Western Church | 83 |
| The Mass reduced to an irrational and unspiritual offering of the Body of Christ | 85 |
| The Protestant idea of the Eucharistic service as for Communion only | 87 |
| This as one-sided as the Roman idea of Eucharistic worship | 90 |
| Mistake in the suppression of the Eucharistic Anaphora | 91 |
| English Mattins and Evensong and the dethronement of the Eucharistic service | 93 |
| Defects of Anglican service derived from Roman service | 94 |
| Mistake to regard the Canonical office as more especially the Worship of God, and the Eucharistic service as more especially the worship of Christ in His sacramental Presence or in His sacramental gift | 97 |
| No room for the distinction of a higher and a lower Christian worship | 99 |
| Mistake to dissociate Eucharistic acts from Eucharistic words or *vice-versâ* | 101 |
| Christian theology can only be upheld by Eucharistic worship | 103 |
| The Roman theory and practice of the Mass opposed to true Eucharistic worship | 106 |

|   |   |
|---|---|
| Mistake to think to restore true Eucharistic worship by the mere adoption of Roman theory and practice .. | 109 |
| A true theory must start from the recognition of the union of the worship of the Church on earth with that of the Church in Heaven .. | 113 |
| It must recognize the truth of Christ's offering in Heaven .. | 114 |
| It must reject the useless mystery of Transubstantiation .. | 115 |
| It must reject the idea of an offering of Christ's Body and Blood by the priest alone or by the mere utterance of words of institution.. | 115 |
| It must recognize the Eucharistic service to be a sacrifice of faith and prayer offered up by the whole Church in union with Christ's intercessory offering of His sacrifice in Heaven .. | 116 |

## Postscript.

### RIVAL PROGRAMMES IN THE CHURCH OF ENGLAND.

|   |   |
|---|---|
| The so-called Catholic programme in "the Lord's Day and the Holy Eucharist" | 118 |
| The Protestant Evangelical programme of Archdeacon Sinclair | 119 |
| Objections to this distinction of parties "sacerdotal" and "Evangelical" | 121 |
| The true "Sacerdotalism" and the false .. | 122 |
| The true "Evangelicalism" and the false | 126 |
| True Evangelicalism not inconsistent, but one with true sacerdotalism | 135 |

# Considerations on Eucharistic Worship.

IT is undoubtedly a crying scandal in a Christian Church, the neglect or denial of the Christian sacrifice of the Eucharist. For whatever view may be entertained as to the nature of this sacrifice, and whether it be a "true and proper" sacrifice from a physical or metaphysical point of view or not, the observance of Christ's Eucharistic institution is the only sacrifice, or substitute for a sacrifice, which the Christian Church has, and which has only swept away all other sacrifices or supposed sacrifices, because it is the reasonable substitute for them, in which whatever true meaning they had is absolutely fulfilled. The observance of Christ's Eucharistic institution is the sacrifice of Christian faith as of Christian worship.

Faith and worship must go together. There cannot be a true Christian faith without a true Christian worship. Christianity is not a mere faith, but a worship, and its worship must be the real and not the mere verbal expression of its faith. "The Catholic faith is this—that we worship one God in Trinity, and Trinity in Unity;" and God is only thus worshipped and truly believed in, when by means of the Eucharistic service of

Christ's appointment, God the Father is worshipped *through* God the Son *in* God the Holy Ghost; *through* God the Son, because through God the Son made man for us, and through the sacrifice which as man He offered and continues to offer; *in* God the Holy Ghost, because in the power of the Holy Ghost proceeding from the sacrifice of Christ to sanctify and unite all disciples of Christ in one holy communion and fellowship. So only is God the Father worshipped in spirit and in truth when He is thus worshipped through God the Son and in God the Holy Ghost.

The observance of Christ's Eucharistic institution is thus the only means of a *real* worship of the Christian God, the living God Who has revealed Himself in and by Christ in His threefold personality of Father, Son, and Holy Ghost, and Who thus lives not only in Himself, but to call us to the participation together of His divine life. The purely verbal worship by the verbal confession of an abstract Triune God is not sufficient to constitute distinctively Christian worship, and does not rise above the level of a Unitarian Deism. The *real* worship by means of the observance of Christ's Eucharistic institution alone constitutes distinctively Christian worship, the worship of Christian theism, as opposed to a Unitarian Deism. Distinctive Christian theology, or a distinctively Christian faith in the mysteries of the Trinity and the Incarnation, thus essentially depends for its justification on the observance of Christ's Eucharistic institution, and without this observance has no proper foundation to rest upon.

And so we find that where avowedly no importance is

attached to the Eucharistic observance as the essential element of Christian worship, there has ceased to be any particular sensitiveness as to the necessity or importance of an orthodox faith in these Christian mysteries of the Trinity and the Incarnation. The traditional formulæ with regard to them may be retained, but they are not insisted on, nor is their true value recognized. They are only retained, because there is no particular reason for giving them up. The ordinary popular Protestantism of England indeed assumes, either expressly or by implication, that there may be a saving faith in Christ and Christ's Atonement without special faith of any kind in the mysteries of the Trinity and the Incarnation. So, on the ground of this unwarrantable assumption, it claims to transform Christianity into a faith which is no worship, or which can dispense with all worship and even with ordinary reverence for sacred things.

But even if we were to let pass this primary assumption of an ignorant, vulgar Protestantism, can there be any justification for its further assumption that faith in Christ and Christ's atonement can dispense with the observance of Christ's Eucharistic institution? Faith in Christ is sheer hypocrisy without the worship of Christ, and is a real worship of Christ possible where there is absolute indifference towards, if not a real contempt for the regular habitual observance of Christ's Eucharistic institution?

Protestantism, moreover, and especially in its characteristically English forms of a conceited aggressive Puritanism and Methodism, has always specially plumed itself on its superior faith in Christ's Atonement. And yet in the last resort what is the only real evidence we have of the truth of Christ's Atonement but Christ's own words in the Eucharistic institution, "This is My Body, which is given for you;" "This is My Blood, which is shed for you, and for many, for the remission of sins?" It was only in the power of these words that the Apostles received authority to preach repentance and remission of sins in the name of Christ. If Christ had not uttered these words, had not thus solemnly declared His intention beforehand to offer the atoning sacrifice, His Passion and Death would not have been the atoning sacrifice, would never have been known to be so. And what is Christ's command of Eucharistic observance but His own sprinkling of His Precious Blood for the sanctification of His future Church in atoning reconciliation with God? And what is every Eucharistic celebration in the bosom of His Church in obedience to His command, but His own continued preaching of the Atoning Power of His Cross and Passion, and His Church's profession of faith in the truth of that preaching?

Moreover, without the Eucharistic celebration there cannot be the full enjoyment of the blessing of Christ's Atonement. For it was the very purpose of the self-sacrifice of Christ in His atoning death, thus to gather together in one in the Eucharistic remembrance of it the scattered children of God, and so make them one flock under Himself the true Shepherd. (John xi. 51, 52.) There is no atonement for Christian people without Christian unity and Christian fellowship (1 John i. 7), and the Eucharistic celebration in the bosom of the Church is the signature of both, not only in themselves, but as the result of Christ's Atonement, and thus it is the only true profession of a Christian faith in the mystery of that Atonement, as we have seen that it is in the mysteries of the Trinity and the Incarnation.

It is to be observed, moreover, that it is all this, as an objective celebration on the part of the Church generally, over and above its further value for subjective individual communion. For Christian worship should be objective and not merely subjective; it should be for the honour of Christ, and not merely for the benefit of the individual Christian. Christ is to be honoured objectively, in the public observance of the Eucharist as His institution, and not merely subjectively, in the subjective observance of individual communion. His honour is not to be subordinated to our individual convenience. The want of a habitual objective observance of Christ's Institution is not sufficiently compensated by the occasional subjective observance by individual communion. Christ is not sufficiently honoured even in the subjective observance, when He is not honoured by the habitual objective observance. We lose the full benefit to ourselves even of individual communion, when we thus subordinate the honour of Christ to our own convenience with regard to the act of communion.

Those who argue from primitive practice against all non-communicating attendance in Eucharistic worship, mistake the letter of primitive practice for the spirit, and ignore the fact that the earlier Church did not therefore presume to substitute a non-Eucharistic worship as the normal or habitual worship of Christian people, nor did it regard Eucharistic worship as solely for communion or as specifically fulfilled by the act of communion only. It is far more in accordance with both the letter and the spirit of primitive practice, as evidenced by ancient liturgies to consider that all Christian worship even apart from Communion, should be offered through the medium of that institution of Christ, which alone makes it truly Christian. To insist that there shall be no objective observance of Christ's institution apart from the individual communion of every member of the Church present at such observance, is simply to create the necessity for the introduction of another worship which is not the true form of Christian worship, but only a miserable substitute. It is, moreover, to exercise a false kind of coercion over Christian consciences with regard to Communion itself, which only tends to ensnare the simple, and taken in conjunction with the absence or neglect of a real moral discipline in the Church, has only led to the greater profanation on the one hand as to the greater contempt on the other.

Mere communion is not the whole end of the Eucharistic observance, but communion is only a further means to worship, and a worshipless communion is even a greater mistake than a communionless worship. And therefore even where the subjective observance of Christ's institution by individual communion is not always practicable or desirable, yet the individual Christian is surely called upon to unite himself with his fellow-members in Christ's Church in the objective observance of Christ's institution by the Church, and not unnecessarily separate himself from them in what alone is the true form and essential element of all Christian worship. A non-Eucharistic worship, that is, a worship which is not based upon the objective observance of Christ's Eucharistic institution, is not a genuine Christian worship, because it is not a sufficient profession of Christian faith in the great Christian mysteries of the Trinity, the Incarnation, the Atonement. The Eucharistic Service, whatever else it is, is the true sacrifice of Christian faith and Christian worship.

It is therefore a crying scandal in a Christian Church, the neglect or denial of this sacrifice of Christian faith and Christian worship, or its relegation to a place of comparative obscurity and unimportance in a system of what professes to be Christian worship. This, however, is the state of affairs which still largely prevails amongst us in the Church of England, and this degradation of Eucharistic service and worship is evidence of the extent to which a jealous Puritanism has fastened its mischievous beak on the very vitals of the Church. And therefore, too, it is not to be wondered at, that some amongst us should think to remedy this unsatisfactory state of affairs with regard to Eucharistic service and worship, by the adoption or re-introduction of or closer approximation to the purely Roman doctrine and practice of the Sacrifice of the Mass.

But as we think to be able to shew this blind admiration of Roman doctrine and practice is a profound mistake. The Roman doctrine and practice of the sacrifice of the Mass has been, and is, as great a scandal to Christendom as the Protestant neglect and denial, and is as great a degradation of Eucharistic service and worship as that which a mischievous Puritanism has inflicted on the Church of England. The one scandal has, in fact, begotten the other. Protestant neglect and denial has only sprung out of Roman misrepresentation and misuse. The Roman sacrifice of the Mass is not the Catholic sacrifice of the Eucharist. The Roman doctrine and practice is not even in accordance with the text of the Canon of the Mass, still less with that of any other ancient liturgy of reputation or authority.

But what is more remarkable is the fact that Roman authorities themselves are not agreed as to the nature of that sacrifice which they assert in the Mass. None of them can give any definite consistent account of it. There are any number of different theories on the subject, which do not in the least approximate to any general common view, but are so violently opposed to one another that if any one of them be in the least true, the others are necessarily wholly false. It is the Jesuit school more especially that has indulged in a most extraordinary liberty of speculation on this subject of the nature of the sacrifice in the Mass, inventing theory after theory, each more ridiculous and extravagant than the other, and all equally insulting to common sense as to Christian faith. The present writer has endeavoured to discuss these Jesuit and other Roman speculations on the nature of the sacrifice of the Mass in a more elaborate treatise awaiting publication. Here he will confine himself to a brief criticism of Roman doctrine and practice generally, as they claim to be founded upon, or justified by, the decrees of the Council of Trent.

Modern High Church or Catholic Anglicans, in their justifiable antipathy to a false Protestantism, which only rends and devours the Church of Christ, have often been disposed to accord a considerable degree of respect to the decisions of the Council of Trent, and to think a healthful re-union between the separated Churches of England and Rome possible on the basis of these decisions. The present writer, as originally a disciple of the late Bishop Forbes, of Brechin, acknowledges himself to have been strongly affected by this influence, and to have cherished a certain degree of prejudice in favour of the entire Catholic orthodoxy and dogmatic value of the decrees of Trent; but a further study, and more especially of Roman writers themselves, has convinced him that these vaunted pronouncements of the Latin Church are not so soundly Catholic and orthodox as they appear or profess, but are as halting and inconsistent in their own way as the Anglican thirty-nine articles are in another way.

Even the famous decree of justification (Sess. vi., cap. 7), which is thought to settle so decisively the whole question, and to effectually dispose of the Protestant contention, may be shewn to be anything but a faithful setting forth of Catholic orthodox truth, may be shewn to be nothing but a series of incoherent, inconsistent statements, in which the real, the essential truth, is not once properly recognized, while the falsehood taught or implied is hidden behind equivocating verbiage and pious platitudes. It is not a faithful setting forth of orthodox Catholic truth; its teaching of the *unica formalis causa* of justification is not only essentially defective, but essentially false, because it leaves out of account an essential point of orthodox Catholic truth, which entirely alters the complexion of the whole doctrine, a point the importance of which is borne witness to, on the confession of Roman theologians themselves, by the orthodox Catholic tradition of Greek theology, while it had been forgotten and ignored by the later tradition of the Latin Church.

The true doctrine, the orthodox Catholic doctrine to which Greek theology bears witness, is justification neither by inherent individual righteousness, as the Council of Trent asserts, nor by the mere imputed righteousness of Christ, as the Protestant contention is but justification by the substantial presence or indwelling of God the Holy Ghost. In the light of this forgotten truth of the divine gift of the substantial presence or indwelling of God the Holy Ghost, the Tridentine doctrine of justification by inherent individual righteousness is seen to be as false as the Protestant doctrine of justification by imputed righteousness.

Indeed, the Protestant doctrine is seen to have something more to say for itself than what it was given credit for, or than the miserably imperfect Tridentine doctrine, which does not even correct the fundamental error of the Protestant, but adopts that error, and only superadds to it a further error of its own, which makes matters worse. For the Council of Trent really adopts the Protestant theory of imputation under the mere disguise of a new name, the communication of merits, and what it asserts is that we are justified not only by the communication of the merits of Christ, but by our own inherent individual righteousness which is the result of that communication, surely a very inconsistent statement of doctrine. It is just this Latin mediæval doctrine of merit that is the foundation of the Protestant theory of imputation. And it is false to say, as the Council of Trent does say, that Christ as Man is only the meritorious cause of our justification, and not the efficient cause. He is only the meritorious cause, as He is at the same time the efficient cause through the Holy Ghost by Whom His Sacred Manhood was anointed to this very end.

Without entering further into the question (on which a great deal more might be said), enough has been said to entitle us to affirm from a perfectly orthodox and Catholic standpoint, that the Tridentine doctrine of justification is essentially defective and false, and that its defects and mistakes arise from the fact that the Latin Church was not competent by itself to decide the Protestant controversy, because by its separation from and loss of living contact with the Eastern Church it had also lost an essential part of Catholic tradition, which alone could enable it to decide the questions at issue in accordance with perfect Catholic orthodoxy.

The case is very much the same as regards the question of the Eucharistic sacrifice. Here too, Tridentine doctrine is essentially defective, and essentially false. It wholly leaves out of account, and thus in effect denies if not explicitly yet by clear implication, the essentially orthodox Catholic truth of Christ's continued offering in

Heaven of the one "true and proper" sacrifice, the sacrifice of the Cross. So far, therefore, from correcting what is really the fundamental error of the Protestant contention, the denial, namely, of a continued offering of the one sacrifice of the Cross by Christ Himself in Heaven, it adopts this very error, only to make matters worse by superadding or grafting on to it a further error of its own, which not only Protestants but orthodox Catholics have every right to reject.

It asserts that Christ only exercises His Melchizedek priesthood through the priesthood of His Church on earth in the sacrifice of the Mass, and that this exercise of His Melchizedek priesthood in the sacrifice of the Mass consists in the offering to God of His Body and Blood under the so-called forms or species of bread and wine, that is, their accidents without their substances. The real falsehood of this doctrine is greatly hidden by the various ambiguities and equivocations in other statements of the Tridentine decree, on which the doctrine professes to depend for its justification, statements several of which are true enough in themselves, but only true on supposition of another than the Tridentine doctrine. The Tridentine doctrine is in fact a counterfeit doctrine which endeavours to appropriate to itself certain features of the true doctrine in order to pass itself off as that very doctrine itself. There is undoubtedly a very close relation between the celebration of the Eucharist by Christ's Church on earth and Christ's own exercise of His Melchizedek priesthood in Heaven. It is the great mistake of Protestantism not to recognize this relation and the true nature of Christ's

Melchizedek priesthood in Heaven. At the same time it is an utter distortion of this relation to assert, as the Council of Trent does, that the Eucharistic celebration itself is Christ's very exercise of His Melchizedek priesthood. Such a statement is wholly false, and contrary to every word of the teaching of the Epistle to the Hebrews. Christ personally exercises His Melchizedek priesthood even in the offering of sacrifice, not on earth but in Heaven. Such is the plain unmistakeable teaching of the Epistle to the Hebrews; Chap. viii. and elsewhere. Romanism equally with Protestantism, and Protestantism equally with Romanism falsify this teaching; Protestantism, by denying that Christ exercises His Melchizedek priesthood in the offering of sacrifice, that is, the continued sacrificial offering of the sacrifice of the Cross ; Romanism, by asserting that He exercises that priesthood by the offering of another sacrifice of His Body and Blood upon earth to take the place of the former sacrifice which is thought to have ceased to be offered, even as the Levitical sacrifices have, to be no longer offered even before God in Heaven as still a true sacrificial offering of Christ's Body and Blood. But if, as Protestant and Romanist equally assert, the sacrifice of the Cross has absolutely ceased to be offered so as not even to be offered by Christ in Heaven, and if as the Romanist asserts, it therefore needs another sacrifice of Christ's Body and Blood to take its place, in neither case is the sacrifice of the Cross that perfect sacrifice which the writer of the Epistle to the Hebrews claims it to be.

And so indeed the Council of Trent begins its decree

on the sacrifice of the Mass, by deliberately misapplying the distinction which the inspired writer of the Epistle to the Hebrews draws between the Levitical priesthood and the priesthood of Christ, in order to make it serve as a basis for the distinction which it draws itself between Christ's priesthood in the offering of the sacrifice of the Cross, and His priesthood in the offering of the sacrifice of the Mass, by which it is made to appear that not Christ's priesthood in the sacrifice of the Cross, but only His priesthood in the sacrifice of the Mass is His perfect priesthood, the offering of the perfect sacrifice. This is indeed to take advantage of the Scriptural argument only in order to discredit the Scriptural conclusion to that argument. What the Council of Trent asserts is that Christ's priesthood is only consummated by the actual repeated offering of a new sacrifice of His Body and Blood in the Mass, to take the place of the former sacrifice of the Cross which it commemorates, represents, and applies, and not by the perpetual offering of that very sacrifice of the Cross immediately before God in Heaven. But the Scriptural conclusion has nothing to do with any new sacrifice of the Mass, but only with the one sacrifice of the Cross, and what the author of the Epistle to the Hebrews asserts and is anxious to establish, is Christ's perfect priesthood in the offering of the one perfect sacrifice of the Cross; a priesthood which is perfect, because it is a perpetual priesthood, whose exercise consists in the perpetual offering of the one abiding sacrifice of Christ's Body and Blood. Christ is a priest for ever, because He offers for ever the very sacrifice by which He obtained that eternal priesthood, for it is by His Passion and Death He has merited His glorious Resurrection and Ascension, and by His Resurrection and Ascension He has obtained His divinely royal priesthood after the order of Melchizedek.

Moreover, the sacrifice of the Cross is only the perfect sacrifice of divine worship and atonement for men as, having been begun to be offered on earth, it continues to be offered for ever in Heaven by one and the same act of offering through one and the same Eternal Spirit, so as to have no need to be supplemented by any further offering of a new sacrifice of Christ's Body and Blood either on earth or in Heaven. The perfection of the sacrifice consists not in its unity alone, but in its perpetuity. The perpetuity of Christ's priesthood implies the perpetuity of His sacrifice, for His priesthood is not a mere titular dignity, but a real priesthood which only exists in the real continuous exercise of its functions. If it is the mistake of Protestants to assert in the sacrifice of Christ unity without perpetuity, it is the mistake of Romanists to assert perpetuity without unity; perpetuity by repetition of another sacrifice, not by continuance of the same sacrifice. Christ, then, is priest for ever only in the perpetual offering of the one true sacrifice of His Body and Blood, the sacrifice of the Cross; not in the offering of any other sacrifice of that Body and Blood. Both His priesthood and His sacrifice, as they are perpetual, so also are they unchangeable or inviolable (ἀπαραβατον, Heb. vii. 24), personal to Himself in the strictest sense, and therefore not a priesthood which He exercises, nor a sacrifice which He offers, as the Roman doctrine asserts, only through the ministry of others, the ministry of His earthly priests.

The ministry of others, the ministry of earthly priests is not required in order to enable Christ to exercise His priesthood and offer His sacrifice, but to enable the Church to take part with Christ in the offering of His sacrifice, which is a very different thing. S. Thomas indeed ventures to maintain that it is not fitting that Christ should receive the effect of His priesthood in Himself, but only that He should communicate it to others, and therefore He is only the fountain of all priesthood, and does not exercise His Melchizedek priesthood Himself, but delegates it wholly to the priesthood of His Church.* This doctrine is radically false, as the present writer has endeavoured to shew in the larger treatise, to which reference has already been made. It is pitiful indeed to see the evasions to which S. Thomas resorts in order to assert that even Christ's Resurrection and Ascension are not the effect or reward of the sacrifice of the Cross.† This is indeed to dishonour Christ under the pretence of honouring Him. And yet it is from this doctrine of S. Thomas, built on so unsound a foundation, that later Roman theologians, and specially those of the Jesuit school, assume, as a theological axiom or commonplace, which does not admit of the least doubt or question and does not require any argument to support it, that Christ does not exercise His Melchizedek priesthood except through the earthly priesthood of His Church.

\* Sum. Theol. P. iii. qu. 22, art. 4.  † Ibid, ad secundum.

The Epistle to the Hebrews teaches the very reverse of this. It teaches that Christ exercises His Melchizedek priesthood in Himself in Heaven, and by the immediate offering before God in Heaven of the one true sacrifice of His Body and Blood, the sacrifice of the Cross. The true Melchizedek offering is no new offering of a new sacrifice of Christ's Body and Blood under the forms of bread and wine, but it is the offering of the very Body and Blood of the sacrifice of the Cross, as by that very offering the true bread and wine of eternal life in the Kingdom of God, and as thus given to us by means of the Eucharistic institution to be our spiritual food and drink. It is only as thus offered by the continued offering of the one sacrifice of the Cross, that the Body and Blood of Christ are in any sense capable of being given to us as our spiritual food and drink, and not by the offering of any new sacrifice of them.

It is to be observed, then, that it is only by a double ambiguity in its statement with regard to Christ's own first Eucharist, that the doctrine of the Council of Trent can plead any justification for itself. Its account of the original Eucharistic institution is this: "Christ declaring Himself as constituted a priest for ever after the order of Melchizedek, offered His Body and Blood to God the Father under the forms of bread and wine, and under the symbols of the same things delivered them to His Apostles, whom He then constituted priests of the New Testament, to receive, and commanded them and their successors in the priesthood to offer, by these words, 'Do this in remembrance of Me,'" etc. Now it is certainly true that by His institution of the Eucharist, Christ did declare Himself as constituted a priest for ever after the order of Melchizedek, true in this sense, namely, that He declared Himself as about to be constituted that priest for ever, first by His Passion, then by His Resurrection and Ascension, for He is no otherwise constituted that priest for ever after the order of Melchizedek, than as through the Eternal Spirit He offered Himself without spot in the sacrifice of the Cross, and as through the same Eternal Spirit of divine holiness and love He was raised from the dead, and declared to be the Son of God with power, "made after the power of an endless life," and also as through the same Spirit He is glorified in His Ascension to be our High-Priestly Advocate and Intercessor with the Father. He did not declare Himself constituted priest for ever after the order of Melchizedek by the Eucharistic institution itself, for He was not so constituted. The Eucharistic institution has no meaning except as it includes the prophecy not only of the Passion, but of the Resurrection and Ascension, and it is only by His Ascension into Heaven that Christ is manifested as the true Priest-King of His Church, that is, the true Melchizedek.

Some Roman theologians indeed maintain that Christ was Melchizedek-priest from the first moment of the Incarnation, because from the first "He was made, not after the law of a carnal commandment, but after the power of an endless life." (Heb. vii. 16.)* But this is surely to confound the potential with the actual, what

* Cf. Thalhofer, Das Opfer des alten und des neuen Bundes. § 20.

Christ from the first had the power to be, with what He actually did become. It is, in fact, to resolve the Incarnate life into a mere phenomenal manifestation or docetic appearance without any substantial reality in every distinct stage of its manifestation, and as it cannot be said that Christ as Man really offered the sacrifice of the Cross before He actually did offer or begin to offer it upon Calvary, as little can it be said that Christ could exercise any functions of Melchizedek priesthood until the Ascension into Heaven. The Melchizedek priesthood, as well as the Resurrection and Ascension, were the reward of a true human obedience on the part of Christ. It is only as He first "learned obedience by the things which He suffered," as He "became obedient unto death, even the death of the Cross," that He has become "the author of eternal salvation to all them that obey Him," and that "God has highly exalted" and set Him at His own right Hand as the Priest-King of His Church. (Heb. v. 8, 9; Phil. ii. 8 *ff.*)

Moreover, it is not even true to say that Christ is "made after the power of an endless life," that is, in the sense of the Apostolic writer, an indissoluble life (κατὰ δύναμιν ζωῆς ἀκαταλύτου), until the Resurrection, for it is only by the Resurrection that Christ has acquired the true indissoluble life in accordance with what S. Paul says, "Christ being raised from the dead, dieth no more; death hath no more dominion over Him. In that He died, He died unto sin once; but in that He liveth, He liveth unto God." This life to God in the Resurrection is that true "power of an endless life" by which Christ is qualified to be "priest for ever after the order of Melchizedek."

Equally mistaken is the view expressed by other modern ultramontane theologians, namely, that Christ already exercised His Melchizedek priesthood in His Passion, a view which does not better, any more than it faithfully adheres to, the doctrine of the Council of Trent, that Christ personally exercised His Melchizedek priesthood only in the Eucharistic institution. As we have seen, however, the Council of Trent only puts forward this view under cover of the ambiguity which there is in its statement that by the Eucharistic institution Christ declared or manifested Himself as constituted priest for ever after the order of Melchizedek. It is true that by the institution of the Eucharist Christ manifested Himself as constituted Melchizedek priest, but not as so constituted by the institution itself, but as to be constituted by all that was to follow, namely, first the Passion, then the Resurrection and Ascension. The Council of Trent prefers to take it that Christ is so constituted by the institution itself altogether apart from the Passion and all that was to follow.

As it is only under cover of an ambiguity in statement, that the Council of Trent can assert that Christ exercises His Melchizedek priesthood only in the sacrifice of the Mass, so also when it asserts that this exercise of Melchizedek priesthood consists in the offering to God of His Body and Blood under the forms of bread and wine. While it is true to say that Christ already in the Eucharistic institution began to offer His Body and Blood to God for the sacrifice of the Cross about to follow, and while also it is true to say that He gave, and expressed His intention to give, His Body and Blood, that is, the Body and Blood of the sacrifice of the Cross, to His disciples by means of, or under the forms of, the Eucharistic bread and wine, it is in no sense true to say that He directly offers His Body and Blood to God under the forms of bread and wine. It is only by a confusion with the truth of the two former statements that the latter statement wins any appearance of truth. The forms of bread and wine are in no sense for the purpose of Christ's offering to God His Body and Blood, but for the purpose of giving that Body and Blood to men, and enabling them to take part with Him in the offering to God of that Body and Blood. Christ had no need then, and has no need now, to offer His Body and Blood under the forms of bread and wine. The offering, that is, the giving of them to men under these forms, is no offering, that is, sacrificing them to God. They are only given to men, as they are previously sacrificed to God. In the first Eucharist, indeed, the sacrifice was only begun, and not complete, or it was complete in Christ's will and intention, though not yet in outward act. But neither in the first Eucharist nor any succeeding, does Christ make any new sacrifice to God of His Body and Blood distinct from that of the Cross.

By the institution of the Eucharist Christ signified and began the offering of His Body and Blood to the sacrifice of the Cross, for it is against all reason and commonsense to interpret, as Roman authorities do, the "given for you" and "shed for you" of the words of institution, as referring to a sacrifice of the Body and Blood in the

Eucharist itself distinct from that of the Cross, and not to the sacrifice of the Cross at all, or to assert as others do, that while they indirectly refer to the sacrifice of the Cross, they directly refer to quite another sacrifice in the Eucharist itself.* Christ's Body was only given for us by the death of the Cross, although as thus given *for* us it is also given *to* us in the Eucharist. So, too, with the Blood of Christ. It was only shed for us in His sacred Passion, though as thus shed *for* us it is also given *to* us in the Eucharist, and given to us as no otherwise shed for us. Roman theory, indeed, by its doctrine of concomitance denies the real gift of the shed blood. The present writer has discussed this part of Roman doctrine at considerable length in his larger treatise and need make no further reference to it here, beyond suggesting that while it makes the words of Christ Himself of none effect, it also makes more difficult of acceptance the idea of a real offering in the Eucharist of Christ's Body and Blood under the forms of bread and wine. Where is the sacrificial offering of Christ's Body when there is no separate offering of the shed Blood?

While then it is true to say, and even truer than what the Council of Trent itself allows, that at the Last Supper Christ delivered to His Apostles to receive, His Body and Blood under the forms of bread and wine, it is not true that by the words, "Do this," He commanded them to offer His Body and Blood under these forms, any more than that He offered them Himself under these forms. He indeed commanded them to offer a sacrifice—the

* See Franzelin, De Euch. Sacr. P. ii. Thes. xi. pp. 339-41.

sacrifice, in the first instance, of their own obedient faith and love, in the taking of bread and wine for the purpose of giving of thanks for Divine redemption, and using His words of blessing upon them to make them the true memorial of His Atoning Death and Passion. At the same time, He would thus enable them to be present with, and to take part in, His own memorial offering of His Death and Passion in that offering of His Body and Blood which He ever makes before God in Heaven. He did not, because He could not, command them simply and directly to offer a sacrifice of His Body and Blood. Such a sacrifice was not immediately in their power, or in the power of anyone but Himself. He could not give to any the power of immediately offering a sacrifice of His Body and Blood when and as they pleased. And how could such a sacrifice be any memorial of His Cross and Passion? He could only give the power of taking part with Him in the offering He Himself perpetually makes. And this it was wholly reasonable that He should call upon all to do who were ready to serve Him in obedient faith and love. So with Him could they make a true memorial before God of His Atoning Death and Passion.

While then it is reasonable, theologically, if not philologically, to interpret " Do this " as equivalent to " offer this sacrifice," it is not " offer this sacrifice of My Body and Blood," but " offer this Eucharistic sacrifice of bread and wine, the sacrifice of your obedient faith and love, so as to take part with Me in the perpetual offering before God of the one true atoning sacrifice of My Body and

Blood, the sacrifice of the Cross." And therefore, even if it may be said that in commanding them to offer the Eucharistic sacrifice of bread and wine, the sacrifice of obedient faith and love, He also indirectly commanded them to offer with Him the sacrifice of His Body and Blood, yet did He not command them to offer another sacrifice of that Body and Blood distinct from that of the Cross, as the Council of Trent asserts or insinuates that He did, a sacrifice of that Body and Blood only under the forms of bread and wine, another sacrifice which is not another. As even in the original Eucharistic institution Christ did not Himself offer any other sacrifice of His Body and Blood but that of the Cross, so did He not, and could not command His Apostles to offer any other sacrifice of them.

It is not true then to say that Christ either personally or by His Church on earth exercises His Melchizedek priesthood by offering a special sacrifice of His Body and Blood under the forms of bread and wine. The Tridentine assertion to this effect rests on a mere confusion of words and ideas. The presence of the mere forms of bread and wine is not the main point in the idea of Christ's fulfilment of the Melchizedek priesthood. Not the earthly forms of bread and wine, but Christ's Body and Blood in themselves, as having been offered by the sacrifice of the Cross, are the true bread and wine of the Melchizedek offering, the offering of the true Melchizedek priest in Heaven.

S. Cyprian seizes the true point of resemblance between the offering of the original and the true Melchizedek when he says, "Christ is the true priest of the Most High God, who in offering His sacrifice to God the Father, offered the same as that of Melchizedek, namely, bread and wine, that is to say, His Body and Blood." He does not say, as Roman doctrine requires us to say, that as Melchizedek offered bread and wine, so Christ offers His Body and Blood under the forms of bread and wine, as if it were these earthly forms, and not the Body and Blood themselves, that constituted the true fulfilment of the Melchizedek offering. It is, moreover, utterly false reasoning to infer, that because Christ gives to us His Body and Blood, the true bread and wine of the Melchizedek offering under the forms of earthly bread and wine, therefore He offers them to God under these forms. He gives them under these forms as already offered and not as still to be offered. He gives them under these forms as already offered in themselves apart from these forms, and at the same time to emphasize the fact of their being as thus already offered the true bread and wine of the Melchizedek offering in Heaven.

So far then as offering is concerned, the Melchizedek priesthood is fulfilled not in any earthly offering, but only in Christ's own heavenly offering. On the other hand, in the Eucharist itself the Melchizedek priesthood is only fulfilled so far as the earthly offering of bread and wine is the means whereby Christ brings forth His offered Body and Blood, to be to us what He has already made them to be in themselves, the bread and wine of eternal life, our spiritual nutriment and refreshment. And it is so that S. Thomas himself regards the matter, as when he says that the priesthood of Melchizedek prefigures the priesthood of Christ more from the point of view of participation of the sacrifice than of oblation, and therefore " in the new law the true sacrifice of Christ is communicated to the faithful under the forms of bread and wine."*

Before leaving this part of Tridentine doctrine it is worth while indeed to notice the serious discrepancy which there is, between the teaching of the Council of Trent and that of S. Thomas on the question of Christ's Melchizedek priesthood, all the more that the Council appears in the first instance simply to base its teaching on that of S. Thomas, and to adopt his phraseology. But it only deals with S. Thomas as it does with the Epistle to the Hebrews. It takes up one half of his teaching, only to discredit the other half. It adopts from S. Thomas the statement of the purpose of Christ's Melchizedek priesthood as being the consummation of the sacrifice of the Cross. It also adopts from S. Thomas the idea that Christ only exercises His Melchizedek priesthood through the earthly priesthood of His Church, that He has only received that priesthood for the purpose of thus communicating it, delegating it in fact, to His Church. But it absolutely contradicts the conclusion of S. Thomas, which is to the effect that since the Melchizedek priesthood is only for the consummating of the sacrifice of the Cross, it has nothing to do with any offering of sacrifice, either of that sacrifice of Christ's Body and Blood or of any other. S. Thomas expressly contrasts Christ's priesthood in the oblation of sacrifice, which is not eternal, but

* Sum. Theol. P. iii. qu. 22, art. 6, ad. 2.

ceased with the sacrifice of Calvary, and His priesthood in the consummation of sacrifice, which is eternal, because it consists in the application of the sacrifice of the Cross in order to the bestowal on men of all the blessings of the life eternal.

Briefly stated, the doctrine of S. Thomas is, Christ's exercise of Melchizedek priesthood consists not in the offering of sacrifice, but only in the application of the sacrifice already offered. If then S. Thomas says that Christ only exercises His Melchizedek priesthood through the priesthood of His Church, he at the same time denies that Christ offers any new sacrifice of His Body and Blood under the forms of bread and wine. On his doctrine the forms of bread and wine are for no offering of another sacrifice, but only for the participation of the true sacrifice of Christ already offered, the sacrifice of the Cross. He thus flatly contradicts beforehand the inexpressibly foolish and absolutely unscriptural doctrine of Bellarmin, and later Jesuit theologians, that participation in the Eucharist is no participation of the sacrifice of the Cross, but participation of a new sacrifice of Christ's Body and Blood in the Mass itself. This later doctrine of the participation is indeed in accordance with the Tridentine doctrine of the sacrifice, of which it is the *reductio ad absurdum*.

If the doctrine of S. Thomas is at fault in not recognizing Christ's exercise of His Melchizedek priesthood in the continued offering of the sacrifice of the Cross, Tridentine doctrine is even more seriously at fault in asserting this exercise of Melchizedek priesthood to consist in the offering of another sacrifice. S. Thomas is at fault in opposing "consummation" to "oblation," but the Council of Trent is doubly wrong in building on S. Thomas' doctrine of consummation its own doctrine of the offering of another sacrifice. Christ's priesthood, as His Sacrifice of the Cross itself, is consummated by the continued offering of the one and the same sacrifice in Heaven, not by any repeated offerings of another sacrifice in its place. His Melchizedek priesthood after His Ascension is not another kind of priesthood, nor essentially different from that priesthood which He exercised previously upon earth, but only its perfection, its higher form, and therefore consists in the glorified offering of the same sacrifice. It would be an altogether new priesthood if it consisted in the offering of another sacrifice. Christ, as priest, is only glorified in the glorified offering of the one sacrifice. As man, He only lives before God in Heaven in the continued offering of the very sacrifice by which He attained that glorified life. His heavenly priesthood is thus in itself absolutely independent of any earthly priesthood of His Church; and it is only a grotesque misrepresentation of the real truth to suggest, as the Council of Trent does, and as later Roman theologians have more unequivocally asserted, that Christ needed to institute an earthly priesthood in order that His own heavenly priesthood might not be extinguished.* He indeed instituted an earthly priesthood in order to bestow on His Church on earth a certain participation in His heavenly priesthood, but it is surely

---

* Quia per mortem sacerdotium ejus extinguendum non erat, etc. Conc. Trid. Sess. xxii.

gross presumption to claim this participation as if it were Christ's own and only exercise of that heavenly priesthood.

To assert also, as the Council of Trent does, that the sacrifice of the Cross needs Christ's own offering of another sacrifice in the Mass in order to consummate it or make it perfect, is surely to assert that the sacrifice of the Cross is in itself essentially imperfect. The derogation is admitted, not palliated, by the assertion that the purpose of the one sacrifice is to apply the fruits of the other. For why should one sacrifice of Christ need another sacrifice of Christ in order to apply its fruits? It is reasonable to assert that the sacrifice of Christ needs a sacrifice also on *our* part in order that we may be able to receive the fruits of Christ's sacrifice, but it is wholly unreasonable to assert that Christ's sacrifice needs another on *His* part in order to His application of the former.

The Tridentine doctrine of the application of the sacrifice of the Cross by the sacrifice of the Mass rests entirely upon this confusion of the sacrifice of the Church with the sacrifice of Christ, and therefore, though it is true to say that Christ also offers the sacrifice of His Church *for* His Church, it is not true to say that He offers His own sacrifice *through* His Church. As then it is false to say that Christ only exercises His Melchizedek priesthood through the priesthood of His Church on earth, so also is it false to say that He exercises this priesthood by the repeated offering on earth of another sacrifice of His Body and Blood under the forms of bread and wine in the Mass, distinct from the sacrifice of the Cross. As observed above, it is only by ambiguities and equivocations that the Council of Trent can plead any justification for its doctrine.

There remain to be noticed some further ambiguities and equivocations by which it endeavours to maintain the immediately propitiatory character of the alleged sacrifice of the Mass as distinct from the sacrifice of the Cross. It is not content to assert the Mass to be propitiatory simply as being the application of the benefits of the sacrifice of the Cross, though it pleads this as an excuse against any supposed derogation from the sacrifice of the Cross. First it takes advantage of the ambiguity attaching to the older language of the Church which describes the Eucharist as the unbloody sacrifice (ἀναίμακτος θυσία) of the Church. Without going too far into the question here, it may be unhesitatingly asserted, that when this language was first used it was for the purpose of contrasting the Church's sacrifice in its outward aspect, with the outward aspect of Jewish and heathen sacrifices, and it had reference, not to any supposed new immolation of Christ's Body and Blood in the Eucharist, but to the Church's unbloody offering of bread and wine. It emphasized the fact of no new shedding of blood being required in order to offer a true sacrifice to God.

It may also, however, be true to say that the Church's offering of bread and wine is a certain unbloody offering of Christ's Body and Blood, so far as the Eucharistic bread and wine are commemorative and representative of the slain Body and shed Blood of the sacrifice of the Cross. But a real unbloody offering of Christ's Body and

Blood, an unbloody immolation of Christ, as the Council of Trent calls it, is a contradiction in terms. Christ only immolated Himself by the shedding of His Precious Blood, and His real offering continued in Heaven itself is not rightly described as an unbloody offering. It is a real offering of His Body *and* Blood, that is, the slain Body and shed Blood of the sacrifice of the Cross, not simply as Roman doctrine asserts, of Christ's Body and Blood together in one another by necessary concomitance. Christ offers His shed Blood as separate, sacrificially at least, from His slain Body. His offering is not, as Roman doctrine asserts, of His Body alone, in which His Blood happens to be contained. The Eucharistic institution itself is Christ's own testimony to a certain abiding sacrificial separateness of His slain Body and shed Blood. If there is any truth at all in the doctrine of the Real Presence, it is only true on supposition of a real distinction between Christ's gift of His living-slain Body and His shed Blood. There is no such a thing then as a real unbloody immolation of Christ in the Mass, for Christ cannot immolate Himself except by the separate sacrificial offering of His shed Blood. His offering indeed is not the shedding of His Blood, but it is the offering of His Blood that has been shed. And it is on the offering of the Blood that everything depends. It is the shed Blood that makes the slain Body a propitiatory sacrifice. If, then, the sacrifice of the Mass is, as the Council of Trent says, an unbloody immolation of Christ, an immolation so-called of the Body of Christ in which the Blood happens to be contained by necessary concomitance, but without any sacrificial separation of that Blood, it is no propitiatory sacrifice.

But all previous ambiguities and equivocations of the Council of Trent are outdone by those which are contained in the passage immediately following, in which, while expressly distinguishing between the sacrifice of the Cross and the sacrifice of the Mass, it seeks to establish absolute identity of propitiatory character by saying, "One and the same is the sacrificial victim, the same Christ now offering by the ministry of His priests, Who once offered Himself upon the Cross, the mode of offering alone being different."* Here are heaped together statements severally true from different points of view, but certainly not true together from one and the same point of view.

The first assertion with regard to the identity of the sacrificial victim is only ambiguously true on supposition of Tridentine doctrine, it is only true as it is the same Christ Who is the sacrificial victim. But if He has ceased to be the sacrificial victim of the sacrifice of the Cross, and only becomes a sacrificial victim in another way by the sacrifice of the Mass, He is not the same sacrificial victim. The Tridentine statement of identity of sacrificial victim is only really true on supposition of other than Tridentine doctrine, only true on supposition of Christ's continued existence as sacrificial victim even in Heaven by reason of His continued offering of the

* Una eademque est hostia, idem nunc offerens sacerdotium ministerio, qui seipsum tunc in cruce obtulit, sola offerendi ratione diversa.

sacrifice of the Cross. It is not true on any other supposition; not true, therefore, on supposition that Christ offers Himself by the ministry of His earthly priests by a new mode of offering different from that of the Cross. On this supposition, Christ as a sacrificial victim in the Mass is not the sacrificial victim of the sacrifice of the Cross, but of the new sacrifice of the Mass itself. It makes no difference to the argument even if it be asserted that Christ, as sacrificial victim by the sacrifice of the Mass, only reproduces Himself as He was sacrificial victim by the sacrifice of the Cross. If the sacrifice present in the Mass is not the very sacrifice of the Cross which Christ offers in Heaven, it is altogether false to say the sacrificial victim is one and the same.

On the other hand it is also true to say that Christ offers by the ministry of His earthly priests, and indeed another sacrifice than that of the Cross, but it is not true to say that the sacrifice which He thus offers is any offering of a sacrifice of His Body and Blood. The sacrifice which He thus offers is only that part of the sacrifice which is distinctively the sacrifice of His Church, the Eucharistic offering of bread and wine, which Christ also offers by uniting it with His own heavenly offering of His Body and Blood, so as to make them the vehicles to us of the presence of that heavenly offering, enabling His Church both to take part in His act of offering, and so partake of His sacrifice offered.

Again, it is also true to say "the mode of offering only is different," but the difference is not in Christ's mode of offering, but between Christ's mode of

c

offering and that of His Church. For while Christ continues to offer the one sacrifice of His Body and Blood by one and the same eternal act of offering through the Eternal Spirit, by which He began to offer on earth, it is only by means of the Eucharistic offering of bread and wine that His Church is privileged to take part in the never-ceasing heavenly offering. While, then, it is true to say that the Church offers the Body and Blood of Christ by means of the Eucharistic bread and wine, it is not true to say that Christ Himself does so. And if it be said that what the Church does, Christ does, since what she does she only does in the power of Christ, it is yet not true that Christ does what the Church does in exactly the same sense as the Church is said to do it. He does not use His Church on earth as the mere physical instrument of His will.

Nor does it follow that because He enables His Church by means of the Eucharistic bread and wine to take part in His heavenly offering of His Body and Blood, that He also limits His own offering thereby. Christ indeed may truly be said to offer with His own heavenly offering of His Body and Blood His Church's offering of the same by her participation in His offering, but it is surely absurd on that account to claim that He only offers through His Church and that the offering of His Church is His own whole offering.

And it is surely a higher privilege to assert for the Church that she simply takes part in Christ's own independent offering in Heaven, than that He only now offers through her whatever offering there is of His Body and Blood. The latter may seem the higher privilege, but is anything but so. It claims for the Church a certain superiority over Christ, but only by reducing Christ to the earthly level of the Church. But the other assertion while it recognizes the true dependence of the Church upon Christ, recognizes also that by this very dependence Christ the heavenly Bridegroom raises His Church, His Bride, to His own heavenly level—the level of true bridal equality with Himself.

To assert that Christ continually humbles Himself anew for the sake of His Church is to mistake the very purpose of His former humiliation on earth. If He humbled Himself by the Passion and Death of the Cross to win the Church for Himself as His Bride, it was that He might exalt her spiritually with Himself in His Resurrection and Ascension and by the sending of the Holy Ghost, to present her in and with Himself immediately before God in Heaven a glorious Church in the glorious offering with Him of the one perfect sacrifice of Divine worship, the glorified offering of His sacrifice of the Cross. Christ has fulfilled all humiliation for His Church in the sacrifice of the Cross, all the humiliation it is possible for Him to fulfil; He can offer no further offering of humiliation. To say that He in any way still humbles Himself for His Church, as by offering a new sacrifice of His Body and Blood under the forms of bread and wine, is to deny both the perfect merit of His previous humiliation and the spiritual power of His present exaltation. Whether the actual Church on earth is always able to perfectly realize her spiritual exaltation in Christ, makes no difference to the fact that by the sending of the Holy Ghost Christ does spiritually exalt His Church even on earth in this present time to His own level of Divine worship and intercession in Heaven. The Church is only the Bride of Christ as the Church on earth is one with the Church in Heaven. To deny the real union in Divine worship of the Church on earth with the Church in Heaven is to deny the spiritual mission of the Holy Ghost. And if Christ has still to humble Himself for the sake of the worship of His Church on earth, there is no real union in Divine worship, of the Church on earth with the Church in Heaven.

There is, however, a condition attached to this union of the Church on earth with the Church in Heaven, the same condition as is attached to the effective carrying out of the spiritual mission of the Holy Ghost. " If ye love Me, keep My commandments." (John xiv. 15, 16.) The condition for the continual sending forth of the Holy Ghost, in order to the spiritual exaltation of the Church on earth in union of divine worship with the Church in Heaven, is the loving obedience of the Church on earth to her heavenly Bridegroom in the faithful observance of that Eucharistic institution He has appointed for her, her faithful obedient offering of the Eucharistic bread and wine as such in remembrance of Him. The equality between bride and bridegroom does not do away with the duty of obedience on the part of the bride. This very obedience is the condition of the perfect equality. The Eucharistic bread and wine have been appointed by Christ for the dutiful obedience of His Church, not for any new humiliation for Himself.

It is wholly false then to say that Christ offers a new sacrifice of His Body and Blood under the forms of bread and wine. This is only to confuse the sacrifice of obedience which Christ requires from His Church on earth, with the sacrifice of divine worship He Himself continues to offer in Heaven for His Church, and also enables her to offer with Him. In Heaven He continues to offer the living Body and Blood of the sacrifice of the Cross to be the bread and wine of eternal life to His Church, and in this consists the exercise of His Melchizedek priesthood. But the earthly bread and wine are for the sacrifice of His Church, not indeed the whole of the Church's sacrifice, but an essential part, though no part whatever of Christ's offering of Himself. The earthly bread and wine have been appointed by Christ, first as an essential part of the Church's sacrifice of obedient faith and love, secondly, to signify that Christ still continues to offer His Body and Blood of His sacrifice of the Cross to be the bread and wine of eternal life to His Church, thirdly, to enable His Church in the power of the Holy Ghost to take part in that heavenly offering, and fourthly, to enable the Church also in the same power of the Holy Ghost to partake of the heavenly sacrifice.

We find, then, that it is equally derogatory to the dignity of the Church as the Bride of Christ, as to Christ the heavenly Bridegroom, derogatory to the Church's participation in the divine worship of Christ and His saints in Heaven, as it is derogatory to the perfect merit of Christ's sacrifice of the Cross by which He has won for His Church this peculiar privilege, to assert that

Christ still humbles Himself on earth to offer a new sacrifice of His Body and Blood through His Church under the forms of bread and wine. Christ does not Himself offer His Body and Blood by two different modes of offering, simply because He grants His Church the privilege of taking part with Him in His one offering. And if Christ also offers the offering which He requires and accepts from His Church, the offering of the bread and wine; this makes no difference to His own offering of His Body and Blood. The two different modes of offering, so-called, are really two different offerings which are united as far as the one becomes the means for the Church's participation in the other. It is this difference of the offering that creates the difference in the mode of offering, for while Christ directly offers His Body and Blood to be the true bread and wine of the true Melchizedek offering, the bread and wine of eternal life to His Church, the Church is only admitted to share in this offering of Christ's Body and Blood in virtue of her own obedient offering of that earthly bread and wine which represents them. The difference in the mode of offering is just the difference between Christ and His Church. It is only by ignoring this fundamental difference between Christ and His Church, and by confusing the Body and Blood of Christ as the true bread and wine of the Melchizedek offering in Heaven with the Church's offering of bread and wine which only represent them, that the Council of Trent draws the wholly erroneous conclusion that Christ only exercises His Melchizedek priesthood in the offering of sacrifice through the priesthood of His Church, and that the sacrifice which He thus offers is a new sacrifice of His Body and Blood under the forms of bread and wine, distinct from the sacrifice of the Cross, and yet falsely alleged to have the same propitiatory character and value.

It remains to notice the further assertion of the Council of Trent, expressed in the form of an Anathema on those who deny it, the assertion, namely, that in the Mass a true and proper sacrifice is offered to God. Here again we have an assertion true enough in itself, but absolutely untrue in the sense in which the Council of Trent must be presumed to understand it in accordance with its own previous doctrine. It is perfectly true that in the Eucharist a true and proper sacrifice is offered to God, and this from a twofold point of view. First, the Eucharistic offering of bread and wine is itself the true and proper sacrifice of the Church's faith and obedience, the only true and proper sacrifice which the Church of herself can offer. There is also offered, however, the true and proper sacrifice of Christ's Body and Blood, namely, that true and proper sacrifice of them which Christ offers in Heaven by continuing to offer the sacrifice of His Cross and Passion, and which He enables His Church to take part with Him in offering by means of the Eucharistic bread and wine.

But the "true and proper sacrifice" of the Council of Trent is neither of these. What, in accordance with its previous doctrine, it must be understood and presumed to assert is that the sacrifice in the Mass, though wholly distinct from the sacrifice of the Cross, is yet an equally true and proper sacrifice of Christ's Body and Blood, or, otherwise expressed, that Christ's offering of His Body and Blood in every Mass by a new mode of offering under the forms of bread and wine is as true and proper a sacrifice of them as the former offering of them upon the Cross. However mistaken then Protestants may be in denying that in the Eucharist a true and proper sacrifice is offered to God, they are not mistaken, but fully justified, in denying that any such sacrifice as the Council of Trent asserts is a true and proper sacrifice of the Body and Blood of Christ. This very assertion of true and proper sacrifice reveals the essential inconsistency of Tridentine doctrine. For it is impossible to assert at one and the same time that the sacrifice of the Mass is a distinct sacrifice of Christ's Body and Blood from the sacrifice of the Cross, and also an equally true and proper sacrifice of that Body and Blood. There can only be one true and proper sacrifice of one and the same thing. The true and proper sacrifice of Christ's Body and Blood is the sacrifice of the Cross. In the Eucharistic institution itself, before the Passion, Christ only offered His Body and Blood, as He then not only signified, but actually began, the offering of the sacrifice of the Cross. In maintaining that the only true and proper sacrifice of the Body and Blood of Christ is the sacrifice of the Cross, Protestants are only contending for orthodox Catholic doctrine which the Council of Trent by implication denies.

Moreover, in asserting another true and proper sacrifice of the Body and Blood of Christ over and above the sacrifice of the Cross, the Council of Trent is not true to the teaching of S. Thomas. Throughout the Summa S. Thomas expressly characterizes the sacrifice of the Cross, in contradistinction to the Eucharist, as being the *verum sacrificium*, the *vera immolatio Christi*. He describes the Eucharist as only the image or commemorative representation of the true *immolatio* of the Passion, which for this very reason he says, may also fittingly enough be spoken of as an *immolatio Christi*, though it is not the true *immolatio*.\* The Eucharist, indeed, is more than that image of the sacrifice of the Cross which S. Thomas recognizes it to be. It is the very presence of that sacrifice as Christ Himself offers it in Heaven.† S. Thomas is mistaken equally with Protestants in thinking that the sacrifice of the Cross is fully offered on the Cross itself. For while on the Cross itself Christ may indeed be said to offer the sacrifice of His life, He only offers the sacrifice of His Death in His risen and ascended life, in which He

---

\* Sum. Theol. P. iii. qu. 47, art. 3; qu. 83, art. 1; qu. 22, art. 6, ad 2.

† The Eucharist is the image of the sacrifice in the outward bread and wine, but the sacrifice itself in the real presence of the Body and Blood. Otherwise expressed, the broken bread and the poured out wine are the image of the broken Body and shed Blood of the Passion, but the Eucharistic Body and Blood are not the image, but the very presence of the sacrifice as Christ continues to offer it for us before God in Heaven. Roman doctrine prefers to assert the whole Eucharistic presence as such to be the mere image, and not the living spiritual reality of the former sacrifice. It thus misunderstands the representative character of the Eucharist by ascribing it to the Body and Blood as such, and not to the bread and wine only. And by ascribing this purely representative character to the Eucharistic Body and Blood, it practically degrades the nature and depreciates the value of the real presence on which it professes to insist so strongly.

also first Himself receives the effect of His sacrifice. The sacrifice of the Cross is not fully offered until the Ascension into Heaven, and being then fully offered continues to be offered, the Resurrection and Ascension also as being the result of the sacrifice previously offered becoming part of the sacrifice which continues to be offered. It is only as thus including all its spiritual results in Christ Himself, that the sacrifice of the Cross is truly acceptable to God. For it is not simply as being the sacrifice of life to death that it is truly acceptable, but as being the triumph of life over death, the sacrifice therefore of a life-giving death.

It is the narrow and imperfect conception of the true nature of the sacrifice of the Cross, united with the denial of its continued offering which has given occasion to, though it does not in the least justify, the Tridentine assertion of another true and proper sacrifice of the Body and Blood of Christ. But by the very nature of the true and proper sacrifice there cannot be another. So even if it were true to say that there is another sacrifice of the Body and Blood of Christ in the Mass under the forms of bread and wine, it cannot be a true and proper sacrifice of that Body and Blood. And it is a very strong argument against any such sacrifice, if it is not a true and proper sacrifice. By this assertion of true and proper sacrifice the Council of Trent simply entangles itself in an insoluble difficulty. For if it cannot definitely point where such a sacrifice is, or how it is possible, its assertion is wholly unwarranted.

Apparently it makes the assertion of "true and

proper sacrifice" on no other ground than its previous assertion of the sacrifice of the Mass having the same propitiatory character as the sacrifice of the Cross. But on what ground did it assert this propitiatory character except on the ground of Christ's presence in the Mass as applying the sacrifice of the Cross? But to say that the sacrifice of the Mass is only the means of applying the propitiatory sacrifice of the Cross is in effect to admit that the sacrifice of the Mass is not in itself a true and proper sacrifice of Christ's Body and Blood.

So far then as Tridentine doctrine goes, the assertion of the sacrifice of the Mass as a true and proper sacrifice of Christ's Body and Blood hangs altogether in the air, and has no proper foundation to rest upon. One may have the less scruple in saying this, since later Roman theology has in fact acknowledged it. This very Canon of the Council of Trent has only been an excuse to later theologians, chiefly of the Jesuit School, to claim for themselves a liberty of speculation with regard to the nature of the alleged sacrifice which is simply astounding in any soi-disant Catholics, who specially arrogate to themselves the profession of orthodoxy (falsely indeed, as this very question shews), and which, to say the least, borders on the irreverent and blasphemous.* These theologians claim this liberty of speculation on the ground that though the Council of Trent has declared the sacrifice of the Mass to be a true and proper sacrifice of Christ's Body and Blood, it has nowhere determined the real nature of this

* As, for instance, in Bellarmin, Lessius, Suarez, De Lugo, Cienfuegos, Franzelin.

true and proper sacrifice.* But what is this but to cast an imputation either upon the good faith or the theological competence of the Council of Trent? For if it did not or could not sufficiently determine the real nature of the alleged true and proper sacrifice, it could have no possible right to call on Protestants to accept its assertion of true and proper sacrifice under pain of anathema for refusing. And what are these speculations, by the very confession of those who have indulged in them, but endeavours to solve the difficulty which the Council of Trent has left unsolved, a difficulty which is in fact insoluble, and which these very endeavours prove it to be, as they at the same time prove the whole Tridentine doctrine on the subject to be as hollow as it is false.

The aim of these Jesuit speculations is to establish a sacrifice of the Body and Blood of Christ in the Mass on the ground of some sacrificial change they are supposed to undergo by reason of their presence under the forms of bread and wine. But not one of the various theories put forward by these audacious speculators can be thought to have even remotely established the fact of any such sacrificial change as they pretend, whether it be described as a sacramental destruction or exinanition of the Body and Blood of Christ, or a sacramental production of them out of the bread and wine, or only a so-called mystical separation which is at the same time admitted to be absolutely unreal. Moreover, if any one of these theories were true, it would not establish a true and proper sacrifice of Christ's Body and Blood. These speculations proceed on the absurd

* See Franzelin, De Euch. Sacr. P. ii. c. 5.

supposition that it is enough that there be change of some kind or other in order to establish true and proper sacrifice. But, pitting the various theories against one another, we may easily confute them all, for the purely demutative change *(mutatio in aliquid deterius)* which some of them assert, is no sacrifice, and the immutative change *(mutatio in aliquid melius)* of the bread and wine, which others assert to be the true sacrifice, is no sacrifice of the Body and Blood of Christ, and none of them venture to assert an immutative change of the Body and Blood themselves.

There is no need to enter here into further discussion of these theories. It is sufficient to appeal to them as bearing witness against the pretensions of the Council of Trent to have set forth a true doctrine of the Eucharistic sacrifice, and more especially as proving the wholly equivocal character of its assertion of true and proper sacrifice, or its inconsistency and hardihood in asserting that to be a true and proper sacrifice of the Body and Blood of Christ, which neither is nor can be anything of the kind. This very assertion of "true and proper sacrifice" only exposes the falsehood of the previous assertion of a new sacrifice of Christ's Body and Blood under the forms of bread and wine. The new sacrifice under the forms of bread and wine cannot be a true and proper sacrifice in the same sense as the sacrifice which it only commemorates and represents. And even if one goes so far as to assert that the new sacrifice is only a certain reproduction of the original sacrifice of the Cross, yet as a mere imitative reproduction it cannot be a true and proper sacrifice in the same sense as the original, and it is absurd to speak of its being a true and proper in some other sense. "True and proper" can only have one sense as applied to one and the same thing. Moreover, however the sacrifice of the Mass may be claimed as an imitative reproduction of the sacrifice of the Cross, it cannot possibly be claimed as a full and exact reproduction. If it were in any sense a full and exact reproduction, it would wholly take the place of the original sacrifice, so as to have no need to be regarded as any commemoration or representation of it. The doctrine of a reproduced sacrifice is at the best a very poor substitute for the truer doctrine of the continued offering of the original sacrifice. It is one thing to assert the presence with or under the Eucharistic bread and wine of Christ's continued offering in Heaven, another thing to assert a new offering by Christ on earth. The former is what the Council of Trent does not assert, but by necessary implication denies. It is also one thing to assert a new act of offering on the part of the Church by means of the Eucharistic bread and wine, another thing to assert a new act of offering on the part of Christ. The new act of offering on the part of the Church is her participation in Christ's eternally abiding act of offering in Heaven, and for this reason cannot possibly constitute a new act of offering on Christ's own part.

Since reference has been made above to the Jesuit theories which, accepting and defending the denial of Christ's continued offering in Heaven, endeavour to determine the nature of the alleged true and proper sacrifice of the Body and Blood of Christ in the sacrifice of the

Mass itself, brief reference may also be made to more recent theories of another kind, put forward by German theological writers—as Döllinger, Thalhofer, Scheeben—which endeavour to amalgamate and reconcile Tridentine doctrine with the truer doctrine of the heavenly offering. For a full discussion of these, as of the other theories, the present writer must again refer to the larger treatise in which he has attempted to deal with the whole subject. It is enough for his present purpose to indicate briefly the relation in which they stand to Tridentine doctrine.

Of the three German writers above-mentioned, Döllinger is the one whose view, as it is set forth in his "Christenthum und Kirche," approximates most to what is here maintained to be the true view. Döllinger's view is only vitiated by his acceptance of the fundamental falsehood of the Tridentine doctrine, and the contradictions in which he thereby entangles himself. While he eloquently sets forth the truth of Christ's independent exercise of His Melchizedek priesthood before God in Heaven, he also thinks it necessary to assert Christ's exercise of that same priesthood on earth through the ministry of the earthly priesthood of His Church, and therefore dependent on that ministry. This is entirely to mistake the purpose of the earthly priesthood. The purpose of the earthly priesthood is not to enable Christ to exercise His own essential priesthood, but to enable His Church to participate in the exercise of that priesthood in Heaven. Döllinger himself recognizes this latter truth, as when he asserts that "the Church's offering is a solemn participation in Christ's abiding act of sacrifice in Heaven;" but he spoils the whole effect of this declaration, and mistakes its true meaning, when he immediately subjoins, by way of explanation, "the earthly reproduction and representation of the sacrifice proceeding in the tabernacle not made with hands."

If the Church's offering is the earthly reproduction of the sacrifice in Heaven, then it is no actual participation in Christ's own abiding act of sacrifice in Heaven. On the other hand, if the Church by her Eucharistic offering of bread and wine is enabled to actually participate in Christ's abiding act of sacrifice in Heaven, the true offering of His Body and Blood of the sacrifice of the Cross, there is no need whatsoever of any supposed earthly reproduction of the heavenly sacrifice. The representation of that heavenly sacrifice is not in the Body and Blood themselves, but in the Eucharistic bread and wine. The Body and Blood as present with the bread and wine are the very presence of the heavenly sacrifice and not its mere representation.

It may be remarked here that Roman as well as Anglican theories of the real presence are essentially defective in a twofold respect. The doctrine of a real presence is worth nothing which does not assert the real presence of the heavenly sacrifice. And that doctrine of the real presence is not the true doctrine, which asserts, not the real heavenly presence, but a reproduced presence on earth. It is this very doctrine of reproduction that has given occasion and excuse for the monstrous Jesuit theories of a new sacrifice which the Body and Blood of Christ are supposed to undergo in virtue of this reproduction. But Christ's presence in the Eucharist is no new presence on earth superadded to His presence in Heaven, it is His gracious manifestation to His Church on earth of His very heavenly presence itself. And this presence is not the mere presence of His Body and Blood, but the presence of His heavenly sacrifice, the sacrifice of the Cross as He now offers it complete before God in Heaven, complete only by His Resurrection from the dead and His Ascension into Heaven.

By the Eucharistic celebration, then, the Church has boldness to enter into the holiest itself, in order to be present with and take part in Christ's perpetual offering of His sacrifice of the Cross as it has been made living and life-giving by His Resurrection and Ascension. The Church can have no need, therefore, to claim to offer on earth any other sacrifice of Christ's Body and Blood than what Christ Himself offers in Heaven. What she offers on earth is only her own Eucharistic offering of bread and wine by means of which she is enabled to be present with and take part in the offering of the heavenly offering. It is not true, then, to say that the Church's offering is any direct offering of Christ's Body and Blood on earth under the forms of bread and wine. It is only true to say that by means of her own direct offering of the Eucharistic bread and wine in a Eucharistic manner she is enabled indirectly to take part in Christ's own direct offering of His Body and Blood immediately before God in Heaven. There is no need, therefore, to assert as Döllinger does, besides Christ's independent exercise of His Melchizedek priesthood in Heaven, by which He ever offers before God the sacrifice of the Cross, another exercise of that priesthood on earth by means of His earthly priesthood, by which He offers an earthly reproduction of His heavenly offering under the forms of bread and wine. There is only an inconsistent amalgamation of Catholic truth with Tridentine falsehood.

There is the same fundamental inconsistency in the views of Thalhofer and Scheeben. But what is even more important to observe with regard to these writers is that this inconsistency is less excusable in them. They are both professed Vaticanists of the strictest type, who are therefore under the strictest of obligations to conform their teaching to that of the Council of Trent. It is difficult, therefore, to see how in the face of the teaching of Trent they can accept and defend the doctrine of Christ's exercise of His Melchizedek priesthood in Heaven. For though the Council of Trent does not expressly condemn such a doctrine, it plainly enough denies it by laying down an opposite doctrine. If words have any meaning, it declares that Christ instituted an earthly priesthood for the offering of the sacrifice of the Mass, in order that His own priesthood might not be extinguished, the implication therefore being that His Melchizedek priesthood only now exists in the earthly priesthood, and but for this would be extinguished. If, however, it may be plausibly contended that all that the Council of Trent means is that Christ's priesthood was not to be extinguished on earth, yet in any case, if at the same time the doctrine of Christ's heavenly offering is in any degree true, the very silence of the Council of Trent with regard to it is fatal to its authority as an interpreter of Catholic truth. If the doctrine of Christ's heavenly offering has that essential importance in connection with the doctrine of the Eucharistic Sacrifice which these writers acknowledge it to have, then the Council of Trent can only be regarded as having been criminally negligent in not clearly setting it forth, in order to the more effectual confutation of what was really uncatholic in the Protestant contention.

These modern assertors, then, of the doctrine of Christ's heavenly offering might appear to be in a dilemma with regard to Tridentine doctrine. However, they altogether ignore any difficulty of this kind, but simply endeavour to accommodate the two doctrines by some kind of artificial though really inconsistent compromise. So Thalhofer, besides adopting what must be regarded as a mistaken theory of the nature of the Sacrifice of the Cross itself, represents the heavenly offering, not as one abiding act of sacrifice by which the Sacrifice of the Cross itself is perfected, but as a continually repeated act of sacrifice in the will of Christ, by which the Sacrifice of the Cross is virtually repeated, and then conceives the Eucharistic consecration as a similar repeated act of Christ exercised on earth concurrently with that which is exercised in Heaven.*

Now besides that this whole idea of a repetition of the sacrifice of the Cross even in the will of Christ is essentially unscriptural, if not also irrational, what need, we might ask, of a double simultaneous repetition, a repetition

* See Thalhofer, Das Opfer des alten und neuen Bundes §§ 29-31, and his more recent work, Liturgik Band i. §§ 14, 15.

on earth in addition to that which is supposed to take place in Heaven? The repetition on earth can only make the repetition in Heaven wholly nugatory and superfluous so far as the Church on earth was concerned. And is it not even possible for Christ to bring His Church into relation with the sacrifice which He continues to offer in Heaven, without repeating the very sacrifice in another form on earth?

Scheeben, on the other hand, rightly rejecting the whole idea of any repetition of the sacrifice of the Cross, and yet not recognizing the heavenly offering as an abiding act of sacrifice but only as the virtual continuance of the sacrifice of the Cross, represents the Eucharistic consecration as quite another act of sacrifice on the part of Christ, whereby, however, He makes present to His Church on earth His heavenly offering, that is, the sacrifice of the Cross as it continues to live on in the heavenly offering.* If indeed Scheeben had been content to assert that the Eucharistic consecration is only the means whereby the heavenly offering, and the sacrifice of the Cross as included in it, is made present to the Church on earth, he would have been wholly right. But he is not content with the assertion of this true and Catholic doctrine of the one sacrifice of the Body and Blood of Christ. He must needs combine with it the false Roman assertion of another distinct sacrifice of the Body and Blood of Christ in the Eucharistic consecration itself, and thereby asserts in fact a double sacrifice of that Body and Blood, one sacrifice indeed the means of making present the other,

* Scheeben Dogmatik Bd. iii. § 272, p. 451.

which just for that reason, if for no other, cannot be identical with that other.

And why should it be thought that Christ cannot make present to His Church on earth the sacrifice of His Body and Blood which He presents before God in Heaven without making another sacrifice of them on earth? And, in fact, can another sacrifice of the same thing make present a previous sacrifice? The new sacrifice cannot at once be a new sacrifice and the mere presence of a previous. This theory of another sacrifice is only put forward for the sake of saving the Roman doctrine of Transubstantiation. For Transubstantiation seems to be superfluous, unless it be made out to be a true and proper sacrifice of Christ's Body and Blood. And this Scheeben, in common with Suarez, asserts it to be. He adopts the sacrificial theory of Suarez, according to which sacrifice is oblation by so-called immutation. But even on this theory Transubstantiation cannot be shewn to be a true sacrifice of Christ's Body and Blood. It is in reality a sacrifice of bread and wine which results in the offering—that is, the mere presentation—of the Body and Blood. It is only the bread and wine that are sacrificially immutated, not the Body and Blood. It is only by confusion of terms and ideas that the sacrificial immutation of the bread and wine can be plausibly represented as being another mode of sacrifice of the Body and Blood.

But is there even any such sacrificial immutation of the bread and wine as is alleged? Scheeben himself furnishes us with the most effectual means of confuting the whole idea. He says this sacrificial immutation is effected by the fire of the Holy Ghost descending from Christ in Heaven upon the Eucharistic bread and wine to consume their earthly substances, and form out of them the Body and Blood of Christ.* Now it may be unhesitatingly affirmed that whatever sacrificial immutation is effected by the spiritual fire of the Holy Ghost is no destruction of physical substances. As little is it any new formation or production of the Body and Blood of Christ. What this spiritual fire of the Holy Ghost as descending from Christ in Heaven does indeed effect, is the real union of the Church's Eucharistic offering of bread and wine with Christ's sacrificial offering of His Body and Blood before God in Heaven—a union without any confusion, or any change of substance or physical mode of existence. By this union there is indeed a certain transfusion of spiritual power whereby the very substances of bread and wine are qualified to be the bearers to us of the heavenly and spiritual Body and Blood of the heavenly and spiritual sacrifice.

While then with Scheeben we assert that the Eucharistic consecration is indeed the means whereby the heavenly sacrifice of Christ is made present to the Church on earth, we also assert that just for this very reason it is itself no sacrifice of Christ's Body and Blood; it is not the distinctive sacrificial act of Christ Himself, but the distinctive sacrificial act of the Church whereby she makes her offering of the Eucharistic bread and wine in obedience to Christ's command, in order to its spiritual union with His

---

* See Scheeben Dogmatik Bd. iii. § 272, p. 451; also his Mysterien des Christenthums, p. 492.

own heavenly offering of His Body and Blood, whereby she is enabled both to take part with Him in the act of heavenly offering and to partake of the sacrifice continually offered.

The theory then of a double sacrifice of Christ's Body and Blood cannot be sustained. Scheeben himself, who asserts it, furnishes us with the means of confuting it. Besides that there is no need of another sacrifice, no other sacrifice of Christ's Body and Blood but that which He continues to offer in Heaven is even possible.

The doctrine of Christ's heavenly offering is wholly incompatible with the Tridentine doctrine of the sacrifice of the Mass. If Christ exercises His Melchizedek priesthood in Heaven in the true offering of the sacrifice of the Cross there perfected, He does not exercise it upon earth merely through an earthly priesthood and in the offering of some other sacrifice of His Body and Blood. It is not Christ Who offers His Body and Blood under the forms of bread and wine. And if the Church herself may be said to do so, yet she does not do so directly, but only indirectly, and in this sense, that the Eucharistic bread and wine are the means whereby the Church is enabled to take part in Christ's heavenly offering of His Body and Blood.

Moreover, the doctrine of Christ's heavenly offering is incompatible even with the doctrine of Transubstantiation, and it is this doctrine of Transubstantiation that has first given the occasion and still gives the excuse for the assertion of another offering of the Body and Blood of Christ under the forms of bread and wine. It is the

Eucharistic bread and wine as such in their full natural being and substance and as thus constituting and expressing the Church's own offering of obedient faith, which are the means whereby the Church is enabled to take part in Christ's heavenly offering. The spiritual power which proceeds from Christ's offering in Heaven is no power for the physical destruction of earthly substance or of any part of the Church's offering as such, but for the elevation and sanctification of the Church's whole offering by its union with the offering of Christ. To assert Transubstantiation is, in fact, to degrade equally the sacrifice of Christ and the sacrifice of His Church. It is to substitute for the true heavenly offering of Christ a false earthly offering and sacrifice. It is also unnecessarily to mutilate the sacrifice of the Church, and at the same time to deny her true participation in the heavenly offering of Christ.

It is as false then to say that the Church directly offers the Body and Blood of Christ under the forms of bread and wine, as to say that Christ does so. The Church must first completely offer her own Eucharistic offering of bread and wine in the Eucharistic consecration, not by any destruction of physical or metaphysical substance, but by offering them for spiritual substantial union with Christ's offering of His Body and Blood immediately before God in Heaven. The Eucharistic consecration is no direct offering of Christ's Body and Blood under the forms of bread and wine, because it is the only direct offering there is of the Eucharistic bread and wine, the full sacrificial offering of them, preliminary to any participation by the Church in

Christ's sacrificial offering of His Body and Blood. If the Church presumptuously claims directly to offer the Body and Blood of Christ under the forms of bread and wine, she only barters away the higher privilege of taking part in Christ's heavenly offering.

It may confidently be affirmed that what is here indicated as the truer doctrine on the subject of the Eucharistic sacrifice is far more in accordance with the plain meaning of the Roman Canon of the Mass itself than Tridentine doctrine is, or any later form of Roman doctrine. In justification of this assertion it is sufficient here to appeal to the prayers, "Supra quæ propitio ac sereno vultu respicere digneris," etc., and "Jube hæc perferri per manus sancti Angeli tui," etc., which obviously refer to the Eucharistic gifts of the bread and wine, and not to the Body and Blood of Christ, and which also imply that the Eucharistic consecration is not fully effected by the mere utterance of the words of Institution, but only by the sacrificial union of the Eucharistic gifts as such in their full natural being and substance, with Christ's sacrificial offering of His Body and Blood in Heaven ("Jube hæc perferri in sublime altare tuum, in conspectu durnæ majestatis tuæ," etc.). If against this be urged the earlier occurrence of the words, "Offerimus . . . . hostiam puram, hostiam sanctam," etc., it is sufficient to reply that these words in no sense indicate the "hostia pura," etc., to be already the Body and Blood of Christ, but rather the reverse; they indicate, as the whole connexion shews, that the Eucharistic bread and wine themselves become the "hostia pura," etc., of the Church's offering in virtue of the utterance of the words of Institution and the consequent memorial in them of the Cross and Passion of Christ, His Resurrection and Ascension. Compare also the application of the words "sanctum sacrificium, immaculatam hostiam" to Melchizedek's own offering of bread and wine.

The artificial explanations which Roman liturgists give to the prayer, "Supra quæ," etc., can only be characterized as pitiable evasions, by which they seek to explain away its only legitimate meaning, as when, for instance, it is said that the Church prays for the Divine acceptance of Christ's Body and Blood so far as her offering of them is concerned, not so far as Christ's own offering is concerned.\* But how does this tally with the assertion that Christ only offers through His Church?

As for the "Jube hæc perferri," etc., Roman liturgists have to confess themselves baffled to give a satisfactory explanation of its meaning which shall be in accordance with the usual Roman dogma.† And yet its meaning is perfectly plain to all, except those whose minds are blinded by a false preconceived consecration and transubstantiation theory, and by their denial of the one true offering of Christ in Heaven. What that prayer of the Church plainly indicates is that the consecration of the Eucharistic offering of bread and wine is only fully effected by its spiritual substantial union with Christ's heavenly offering of His Body and Blood, by which the Eucharistic bread and wine become the true communion of the heavenly

\* Cf. Thalhofer Liturgik Bd. i. § 15, 4 b.
† See Hoppe Die Epiklesis u.s.w. pp. 98 *ff.*

Body and Blood, and the means of the Church's fulfilment with all heavenly benediction and grace ("ut quotquot ex hac altaris participatione sacrosanctum Filii tui Corpus et Sanguinem sumpserimus, omni benedictione cœlesti et gratia repleamur").

It is not merely Roman doctrine that is not in accordance with either the letter or the spirit of the Roman Canon of the Mass, but Roman practice. Roman practice may indeed be in accordance with the later rubrics, but it is not in accordance with the more venerable text. It is more especially the secret recitation of the Canon which has given occasion to all the other evils of Roman doctrine and practice. This practice of the secret recitation of the Canon by the priest, belies the whole meaning and purpose of the Canon. It has first obscured the witness which the Canon itself bears to the true doctrine of the Eucharistic sacrifice, and it has then given occasion to all the false opinions with regard to the nature and purpose of the Eucharistic consecration, and of Eucharistic worship generally, which have discredited, and still effectually discredit, the pretensions of the Church of Rome to be even a faithful interpreter of ecclesiastical tradition, to say nothing of its claim to be an infallible teacher of divine truth.* When Roman liturgists, with an air of profound wisdom and authority, tell us that "the priest alone enters

* It is, indeed, by the claim to be the infallible teacher of Divine truth the Roman Church conceals its inability to interpret aright its own liturgical tradition. And yet, if it cannot interpret aright its own liturgical tradition, if it cannot authoritatively declare the true nature of the Eucharistic sacrifice, it cannot be the infallible teacher of Divine truth.

into the Canon" (solus intrat Canonem) as into the Holy of Holies, in order to offer the mysterious sacrifice, and that he offers it, not *nomine populi*, but as the visible representative of Christ, and therefore *secretus vel segregatus a populo*,* they say what every word of the Canon expressly contradicts. Every line of the Canon implies that the priest does not offer alone, does not enter into the Canon alone, but with the people—("Te igitur supplices rogamus . . . quæ tibi offerimus . . . qui tibi offerunt hoc sacrificium laudis, pro se," etc.)—and that he does not offer as the visible representative of Christ, but as the representative and in the name of the people ("Nobis quoque peccatoribus, etc., hanc oblationem servitutis nostræ sed et cunctæ familiæ tuæ," etc.).

What are the so-called prefaces before the Canon but the expression of the union of the Church on earth with the Church in Heaven, in the offering of the sacrifice of praise and thanksgiving for the divine redemption in Christ? These so-called prefaces have only been arbitrarily separated from the Canon by reason of their being variable, while the Canon remains invariable. But there is no more reason for saying the Canon *secreto* than for saying these prefaces *secreto*. Both prefaces and Canon form the true Anaphora or offering of the Eucharistic sacrifice. That offering begins with the Vere Dignum, and the real preface is only the Sursum Corda and Gratias Agamus with their respective responses, by which the faithful are summoned to unite themselves with the

---

* See Thalhofer Liturgik Bd. i. § 28, 36; also Gihr, Das heilige Messopfer, § 56.

officiating priest for the entrance into the Holiest, and the offering there both of her own sacrifice of praise and prayer, and the Sacrifice of Christ.

The Canon was thus never intended to be the private prayer of the priest alone, but the public prayer of the Church, uttered indeed by the ministering priest, but in the hearing of the Church, and as speaking for the Church, as its very first words, especially when taken in conjunction with what immediately precedes, sufficiently indicate, " Te igitur .... supplices rogamus." The effect of the secret recitation of the Canon is therefore to deprive the Church of her due share in that which alone is her proper service and worship of God, the Eucharistic Anaphora, the offering of the true sacrifice of praise and prayer to God. The practice, indeed, has arisen out of a mistaken feeling of reverence, a false reverence which has become the grossest irreverence, a real insult to the Church of God and the virtual suppression of what alone is the Church's true service and worship of God.

Nor is this suppression of the true Eucharistic service atoned for or compensated by the provision of other prayers and devotions, or by any mere subjective devotion on the part of the people, or so-called union of intention with the priest. If the public Eucharistic prayer may be said *secreto*, no other prayer need be said aloud, and the service of God may be all dumb show. In any case it is of no consequence to say any other prayer in Church but the public Eucharistic prayer. The Canon, indeed, may as well be expunged from the Missal as merely retained as a venerable relic of past ages, or enshrined in the dumb show of a false ceremonial which contravenes it at every point.

The secret recitation of the Canon is not only repugnant to its letter and spirit, but it is just this which has given rise to the false ideas with regard to the nature and meaning of Eucharistic consecration and Eucharistic worship generally. The Canon is treated as if it were for no other purpose than the utterance of the words of consecration so-called, and as if the Eucharistic consecration were effected by that utterance and by nothing else. And then the Eucharistic consecration is supposed to consist in the immediate production of the Body and Blood of Christ, in consequence of that utterance, underneath the the so-called forms only of bread and wine. The consecration is thus no consecration of the real bread and wine, but only of their sensible but unsubstantial forms and qualities, by reason of their mere external union with the Body and Blood. Needless to repeat, there is nothing in the Canon to indicate the alleged disappearance of real substances, but everything to indicate the reverse. But what is more important here to observe, the Canon plainly indicates that the consecration is not fully effected by the mere utterance of the words of institution, since even after that utterance various prayers still follow for the acceptance of the offering. The consecration cannot be regarded as fully effected except by the divine acceptance, and the divine acceptance cannot be claimed on the ground of the mere utterance of the sacred words.

The Canon teaches us to distinguish between the

consecration as it is effected by the Church, and as it is effected by God. The consecration as it is effected by the Church is not the consecration as it is effected by God. The consecration as it is effected by the Church consists in the Eucharistic offering of the bread and wine as such, by the utterance over them of the words of Christ, coupled with the Church's prayers for the divine acceptance of her offering; first its acceptance generally ("Quam oblationem .... benedictam, .... acceptabilemque facere digneris ...." *Cf.* also the Supra quæ, etc.); next, its acceptance in order to its living spiritual union with Christ's sacrificial offering of His Body and Blood in Heaven ("jube hæc perferri .... in sublime altare tuum"), and this in order to the transfusion of that spiritual power from the heavenly sacrifice to the earthly, by which the earthly may be the means of a true participation of the heavenly ("ut quotquot," etc.), a transfusion which is something very different from any transubstantiation, whether of the vulgar or the philosophic kind.

The utterance, then, of the sacred words is the true offering of the bread and wine as such, not the immediate offering of Christ's Body and Blood. The Eucharistic bread and wine are not truly offered by any mere preparatory oblations of the offertory, for then there would be no need still to pray in the Canon itself ("quam oblationem .... benedictam .... acceptabilemque facere digneris," etc.). They are only truly, that is sacrificially, offered, so far as the Church can so offer them, by the utterance of the sacred words of Christ, by which even as bread and wine they become the sacrificial memorial of Christ's Death and Passion. And this is not the whole offering even of the bread and wine, for Christ must also offer them on the heavenly altar, by spiritually uniting them with His own offering in Heaven. Except as the Eucharistic bread and wine as such are thus sacrificially united with the offering of Christ in Heaven, there can be no offering by the Church on earth of Christ's Body and Blood.

The Church's offering is her participation with Christ in His heavenly act of offering. But the full consecration of the Eucharistic bread and wine does not consist just in their thus becoming the means of the Church's participation in Christ's heavenly act of offering, but in their being made the vehicles for the true communion of the sacrifice which is ever offered in Heaven. They are so made by the power of God—that is, by the power of the Holy Ghost proceeding from the sacrifice with which they are spiritually united. But, even so, they are only the vehicles for the true communion of the Body and Blood, not themselves the whole communion of that Body and Blood. The communion of the Body and Blood is something more than the communion of the bread and wine, although it is only the communion of the bread and wine that leads to or makes possible the true communion of the Body and Blood. The communion of the Body and Blood is something that continues, or may continue, after the communion of the Eucharistic bread and wine.

In accordance, however, with their Transubstantiation doctrine, Roman theorists tell us that the real communion of the Body and Blood of Christ only continues so long as the species of bread and wine remain unconsumed in the receiver of the sacrament. They tell us that the Body and Blood, even as truly received, necessarily pass away with the passing away of the sacramental species.* This doctrine is a real degradation of the true idea of sacramental communion and a falsification of the teaching contained in John vi. 53-58. If the Body and Blood of Christ as received in or by Christ's sacrament are the true source to us of that eternal life of which Christ speaks, they are so only as having in themselves that eternal life even as they are present in the sacrament, they can only communicate that eternal life as they are capable of truly and substantially remaining in him who truly receives them by means of the Eucharistic bread and wine.

The gloss which some Roman writers are not ashamed to put upon the words of Christ, "My Flesh is meat indeed, and My Blood drink indeed," to the effect that Christ's Flesh and Blood are only that meat and drink as they are reduced to a sacramental state of food and drink under and by means of the species, is as ridiculous as it is false.† If it were true, then Christ's Flesh and Blood would in

---

\* See *e.g.* Lessius De Perfectionibus divinis lib. xii. c. xvi. : "Sextum miraculum est Corporis Christi ad corruptionem specierum desitio in Sacramento." Bellarmin and De Lugo regard this so-called Sacramental destruction of the Body of Christ as a real part of the "true and proper" sacrifice.

† See Franzelin De Euch. Sacr. P. i. Thes. xviii. : "Caro mea vere est cibus et sanguis meus vere est potus," in quo tamen statu Corpus Christi non est, nisi quatenus constitutum sub his visibilibus speciebus. And as to what he means by the "constitutum sub his speciebus," see P. ii. Thes. xvi.

no sense be the meat and drink of eternal life. Transubstantiation, in fact, in the Roman sense, makes impossible a true communion of the true Body and Blood of Christ. It absolutely limits the communion of the Body and Blood of Christ by the concurrent communion of the species. On the other hand, on the true doctrine we have that true Transubstantiation of which the Roman doctrine is the counterfeit. There is no passing away of substance without the passing away of accidents. In the act of communion the whole being and substance of the bread and wine does pass away, in a certain sense, into the being and substance of the Body and Blood of Christ, according to the capacity of the individual Christian to receive these latter. The substances of the bread and wine pass away with their accidents, but leave behind the presence of the Body and Blood of Christ in those who are qualified to retain and enjoy that presence.

There is this true transubstantiation in the faithful communicant, and according to the proportion of his faith and love. But as regards the unfaithful or unworthy communicant, what is true with regard to the coming of the Holy Spirit is also true with regard to the coming of the Body and Blood of Christ in the power of the same Spirit: "Into a malicious soul wisdom shall not enter, nor dwell in the body that is subject unto sin, for the holy Spirit of discipline will flee deceit, and remove from thoughts that are without understanding, and will not abide when unrighteousness cometh in." (Wisd. i. 4, 5.) And therefore it is true to say that, though the Body and Blood of Christ are present with the bread and wine for reception, and are so far received by the reception of the bread and wine, yet they are not truly partaken of; and the assertion of the English Article xxix. is wholly justified, that "the wicked and such as be devoid of a lively faith, although they do carnally and visibly press with their teeth (as S. Augustine saith) the sacrament of the Body and Blood of Christ, yet in no wise are they partakers of Christ; but rather to their condemnation do eat and drink the sign or sacrament of so great a thing." The wicked do not partake of the Body and Blood of Christ "in the use of the Lord's Supper."

Nor does this contradict a true doctrine of the real presence. The presence is there, even if it be rejected. It is not physically tied to the so-called accidents, so as to undergo in any sense what they undergo, or necessarily to pass away just when they pass away. If it passes away, it passes away for quite other reasons than the passing away of the species. If the presence passes away, it passes away because it has been rejected or because of the moral inability to receive or retain it. The presence is not tied to, but associated with the bread and wine, for the purpose of communicating itself by means of them. It remains, therefore, or is capable of remaining, even when the earthly vehicles of its communication have passed away. It remains according to the spiritual power of the receiver to retain and enjoy it, and according to the intensity and sincerity of the act of reception. There is no need then to draw subtle distinctions, as Dr. Pusey does,*

* See his Real Presence the doctrine of the English Church, chap. iii.

between the partaking of Christ and the partaking of the Body and Blood of Christ. The partaking of the Body and Blood of Christ is the partaking of Christ, but the partaking of the bread and wine is not necessarily the partaking of the Body and Blood of Christ. The partaking of the bread and wine is in order to the partaking of the Body and Blood of Christ by means of them, and the guilt of unworthy communion lies not in the partaking of the Body and Blood of Christ, but in the refusal to do so. (*Cf.* Heb. x. 29.)

The Roman transubstantiation then is not the true transubstantiation, but its counterfeit. The Roman doctrine is transubstantiation by consecration merely, that is, by the utterance of the words of consecration. The true doctrine is transubstantiation in real communion, that is, the transubstantiation of the transitory substances of bread and wine into the abiding substance of the Body and Blood of Christ in the faithful receiver. Whatever apparent advantage the Roman transubstantiation doctrine may have for maintaining and securing the doctrine of the real presence, is altogether outweighed by the damage it inflicts upon the doctrine of the sacrifice and of communion, making wholly impossible, as it does, either the true sacrifice of the true Body and Blood of Christ, or a true communion. It is only the virtual suppression of the Eucharistic Canon except the words of consecration which has led to this result, the substitution of the false idea of an impossible transubstantiation by consecration merely, for the true idea of that actual transubstantiation which takes place in faithful communion, the passing away of the earthly presence of the Eucharistic bread and wine into the abiding heavenly presence of the Body and Blood.

Moreover, this suppression of the Canon, coupled with the false idea of transubstantiation by the utterance of the words of consecration only, has prejudicially affected the whole idea of Eucharistic worship. The original and essential idea of Eucharistic worship is that which is expressed at the very beginning of the Eucharistic Anaphora in all Catholic liturgies by the Sursum Corda, or words equivalent, and the Ideo cum angelis, namely, the real union of the Church on earth with the Church in Heaven in the immediate worship of God in Heaven, though Jesus Christ, the heavenly High Priest of the Christian profession, and as being such, the Mediator also of the New Covenant between God and Man, the same idea which is expressed in Heb. xii. 22-29 and x. 19-25. The Eucharistic Anaphora itself is this worship, that is, it is first, the real union of the worship of the Church on earth with the worship of the Church in Heaven, and because it is this, it is also the true and immediate worship of God in Heaven by the Church on earth through Christ in Heaven and His High-Priestly offering of the one perfect sacrifice which alone is acceptable to God, and whose acceptableness is manifested by its very presence and continued offering in Heaven. Eucharistic worship, that is the true Eucharistic worship, is thus the worship of the Father in Spirit and in truth through the only-begotten Son, Who by the eternal sprinkling of His sacrificial Blood purifies our consciences to enable us thus to serve acceptably the living God in one holy fellowship of divine love.

The Eucharistic Anaphora is this worship, and alone properly this worship. But it is this worship only as it is the public worship of the Church, and not the private worship of the earthly priest. It is not the earthly priest who alone is made worthy to immediately approach God in the true Eucharistic worship of God. The priest himself cannot offer this worship except with and through the Church. And if he cannot offer it except *with* and *through* the Church, he cannot offer it alone *for* the Church. Nor is the Church called upon to unite herself merely subjectively with the priest, but rather it is the priest who is called upon to unite himself objectively with the Church. It is the whole Church that is qualified to immediately approach God in Eucharistic service and worship, and the priest is only her public spokesman.

If the subjective worship of God is sufficient for the Church, then Protestantism only draws the right conclusion when it makes the whole worship of God purely subjective. God may as well be subjectively worshipped immediately through Christ in Heaven, as mediately through an earthly priest. It is Romanism itself which is directly responsible for having introduced into the idea of the true worship of God that pure subjectivism of Protestantism which has for the time being overthrown the true idea of the Christian Church and of proper Christian worship. Protestant subjectivism in the worship of God is in any case preferable to the false objectivism of worship which Romanism has developed in another direction. For while, both in theory and practice, excluding the people from the immediate objective worship of God in the Eucharistic Anaphora, the true proper Christian worship of God as such, the Roman Church has been obliged to make up for this by first permitting, then encouraging and justifying, the immediate objective worship of Mary and the Saints, and of their images, which has often practically superseded even the subjective worship of God. There is, indeed, a certain worship or veneration of the Church Triumphant by the Church on earth which is not only justifiable, but even laudable; that, namely, which is in immediate connection with the proper direct worship of God in the Eucharistic Anaphora, to which expression is given in the "Communicantes et memoriam venerantes" of the Roman Missal; but this is very different from that immediate worship of individual saints, altogether apart from Eucharistic worship, and simply before and by means of their images, which is so prominent a feature of modern Roman worship. That worship of the saints is wholly to be rejected, which is not the worship of the communion of the saints in Christ. By the virtual suppression of the Canon, the Roman Church has not only excluded the people from the true objective worship of God by Christ, but also from the true worship of the communion of saints in Christ; and if this suppression has given rise to false subjectivism of the worship of God in Protestantism, it has also given rise to a false objectivism in the worship of saints which is even more objectionable than the false subjectivisim of Protestantism. In all this false objectivism of Roman Saint and Image worship, and of Sacred and Immaculate Heart devotions, false subjectivism is as rampant as in the wildest Protestantism. God is as little glorified with one mind and with one mouth in the one way as in the other. If the true idea of Eucharistic worship, and the true form of Eucharistic service, had always been retained in the Roman Church, there would have been as little reason for these various forms of vulgar devotion as there would have been little excuse for the exclusive subjectivism of Protestantism.

But a further charge to be brought against Roman practice is this, that it supersedes not only the worship of God, but the worship of the heavenly Christ, by the worship of a supposititious sacramental Christ. By the suppression of the Canon in its public aspect, its recitation is naturally regarded as wholly subsidiary to the supposed production of the Body and Blood of Christ by the mere utterance of the words of consecration. The whole interest of the Canon, for either priest or people, is made to centre in that and in nothing else. Both priest and people are called to the worship, not of Christ as in our flesh the great High Priest in Heaven offering His very sacrifice of the Cross for us, but of a sacramental Christ—Christ in a new sacramental mode of existence, as it is called, distinct from His heavenly mode of existence—Christ as a new sacrificial victim upon the earthly altar, representing indeed His former sacrifice, or even His present sacrifice in Heaven, but yet not that very sacrifice itself.

Now of course it may be said that Christ is truly worshipped even as the heavenly priest by being thus worshipped in His sacramental presence. But this only amounts to saying that the objective worship of the sacramental Christ may be a means of the subjective worship of the heavenly Christ. It still remains true that the objective worship of the sacramental Christ is not the objective worship of the heavenly Christ, but a real hindrance to the same and a wholly unnecessary substitute. Christ is only now truly worshipped when He is directly and objectively worshipped in His heavenly glory as our High Priest in Heaven, still offering for us His sacrifice of the Cross. He is only truly worshipped as He Himself as Man still worships God for us in the continual offering of His sacrifice, and as He also at the same time enables us in Him to worship the Father in Spirit and in truth. And therefore is He truly worshipped by His Church on earth in the Eucharistic celebration in which He manifests Himself as in His heavenly presence, offering the heavenly sacrifice for us, and enabling us to offer it with Him. The sacramental presence is no presence distinct from the heavenly presence, but only the manifestation of that presence.

This, indeed, is the true purport of the liturgical invocation of the Holy Ghost in Eastern liturgies, which, though left out in the Roman, is yet implied in the *jube hæc perferri*. The invocation is for no new production so-called of the Body and Blood of Christ any more than the words of consecration are. As the words of consecration are the true offering of the bread and wine in order to their union with Christ's own sacrificial offering of His Body and Blood in Heaven, so the invocation of the

Holy Ghost is in order to the manifestation of this union, the presence of the heavenly offering with the earthly, or as we may perhaps otherwise express the same thing, in order to the transfusion of spiritual power to the earthly offering that it may be the vehicle of the presence and communication of the heavenly. And in accordance with this view of the purport of the Invocation, we find that in the most approved liturgies it is immediately followed by the proper Eucharistic intercession, which is present, in principle at least, even in the Roman rite, in the greatly curtailed form of the Commemoratio pro defunctis and the "nobis quoque peccatoribus," and which is fittingly concluded and summed up in the solemn public recitation of the Lord's prayer by priest and people together (in the Roman rite, wrongly, by priest alone).

Then indeed after that worship of the Father in Spirit and in truth through the Only-Begotten Son, to which expression is given by the solemn public recitation of "Our Father," there naturally follows the special adoration of the heavenly priest Himself in the offering of His heavenly sacrifice, to which expression is given in the Agnus Dei, or by the Sancta Sanctis with the liturgical rites of Fraction and Commixture following. Here, as the Greek rites indicate, is the proper moment for elevation and adoration, and not, as in the modern Roman rite, after the mere utterance of the words of consecration. And the adoration is not of any sacramental presence as such, distinct from the heavenly presence. It is of the heavenly presence as sacramentally manifested, that presence of the heavenly priest offering the heavenly sacrifice which the Agnus Dei indicates. The consecration of the bread and wine, therefore, is not to be conceived as the immediate bringing down of the Body and Blood of Christ from Heaven to earth by the mere utterance of the words of institution, but as the means of raising the minds and hearts of the faithful by the power of the Holy Ghost to the very presence of Christ our High Priest before the throne of God in Heaven, to take part in the heavenly offering, and to partake of the heavenly sacrifice.

It is, however, to be observed that the Holy Ghost does not raise the minds and hearts of the faithful to the heavenly presence of Christ's Body and Blood by turning them from the earthly presence of the sacramental bread and wine. The Holy Ghost only enables the faithful to realize the heavenly presence by at the same time transfusing into the earthly presence of the Eucharistic bread and wine that spiritual power by which it becomes the true vehicle of the manifestation and communion of the heavenly presence, the means of the Church's participation both in the heavenly act of offering and the sacrifice offered. The true consecration of the Eucharistic bread and wine cannot therefore be conceived as effected by the mere utterance of the sacred words of institution, but by the power of the Holy Ghost expressly or implicitly invoked by the Church to unite the earthly offering and sacrifice with the heavenly, and to manifest this union so as to make both sacrifices—the distinctive sacrifice of the Church on earth, and the distinctive sacrifice of Christ in Heaven—truly effective for the purposes for which they are respectively and jointly offered. And as the earthly presence and offering of the bread and wine are not the means for a mere subjective manifestation of the heavenly presence and offering of Christ's Body and Blood, but for a true objective manifestation, so are they the means of a true objective worship of Christ, our great High Priest in Heaven, as they are also the means of a true objective worship of God through Him—the worship of the Father in Spirit and in truth.

If then the Roman theory asserts and requires the objective worship of a sacramental Christ, it denies and hinders the objective worship of the heavenly Christ. It substitutes the former for the latter, and this substitution is no wise justified or excused by the further assertion that the objective worship of the sacramental Christ is, or the fact that it may be, the means of a true subjective worship of the heavenly Christ. Protestantism may equally, if not with even better right, claim justification and excuse for its assertion and attempted practice of a direct subjective worship of God and of Christ, or even of God only, without the worship and mediation of the Man Christ Jesus. A direct subjective worship may justifiably seem preferable to what is acknowledged to be only an indirect subjective worship. And if the objective worship itself is only regarded as the means to the higher subjective worship of the true and final object of worship, it may justifiably or excusably be rejected, if it is found by experience to be more of a hindrance than a help to the admitted higher worship. The case is very different when we conceive the objective worship to be the direct worship of the true and final object of worship, and no mere intermediary worship. For then the subjective worship is not the higher worship, but only subsidiary to the objective.

We see then how Roman practice has vitiated the true idea of Eucharistic worship, its original and essential idea. By the secret recitation of the greater and really important part of the so-called Canon of the Mass, it practically excludes, and indeed proceeds on the principle of excluding, the people from that which is and ought to be the whole Church's true and immediate worship of God through Christ. And then by the concentration of the whole interest of the Canon on the priest's mere utterance of the words of consecration, it transforms Eucharistic worship into the mere worship of a sacramental Christ, and substitutes this for the direct worship of the heavenly Christ, the true High Priest of the Christian profession. It does this in defiance of the Canon itself, every word and line of which testifies to quite another theory of its meaning and purpose than what this practice assumes. It treats the Canon in fact as a dead letter, which is only useful, partly as an occasion for the subjective devotion of the priest celebrating, partly for the retention of a ceremonial which has lost the greater part of its original meaning.

We may also observe how Roman theory and practice with regard to the Canon of the Mass have injuriously affected the whole structure of the Eucharistic service otherwise, and have thus accelerated that tendency to subjectify the whole worship of God, which has reached its extreme limits in some forms of Protestantism. It has been maintained above that the Eucharistic Anaphora is, in its original and essential idea, the true objective worship of God by the Church, both as it is the means of a common worship by the Church on earth with the Church in Heaven, and also as it is the true worship of God through Christ in Heaven, the glorious High Priest of the Christian profession, through Whom alone we can approach the Father to worship Him in spirit and in truth. The Eucharistic Anaphora was thus the only "true and proper" common prayer of the Church, or, at least, the only "true and proper offering" up of that prayer. And so in the ancient liturgies, while the subjects of the Eucharistic intercession were all specified beforehand in the so-called Ectene or Deacon's bidding prayer, the Eucharistic intercession itself after the invocation of the Holy Ghost was alone regarded as the true offering up of those supplications and prayers. But in course of time, in the Western Church more especially, the Eucharistic intercession has been more and more curtailed, and partly broken up and displaced, while the Deacon's bidding prayer has been elaborated into a separate form of responsive service for clergy and people which has been gradually extruded from the Liturgy proper, with the exception of the Kyrie Eleison and the concluding Collect or Collects. (There is the relic of an older use in the Missal service for Good Friday, in which some parts of the original Bidding prayer obviously remain in their proper place.)

This process of liturgical development has undoubtedly

tended to the growth of the purely subjective idea even of public prayer at the expense of that objective idea which is implied in the original practice of the Eucharistic intercession. Not only is the Church formally excluded by means of the secret recitation of the Canon from all real share in the objective offering of the Eucharistic intercession, but public prayer generally is reduced to a minimum in the Eucharistic service, it is practically limited to the Kyrie Eleison and the special collect or collects for the day. And this extrusion of real public prayer from the Eucharistic service is not atoned for by the substitution of a purely individual subjective devotion in connection with the worship of the sacramental Christ, nor by the introduction of other public devotions of a more or less objectionable type in connection with the worship of Mary.

Besides the Eucharistic prayer of thanksgiving, supplication, intercession, which constitutes the Anaphora of the Eucharistic service, or the means by which the Church as one whole takes part in Christ's heavenly offering, the Eucharistic service mainly consists of Scripture lections and psalms, which are by no means to be regarded as a merely accidental, but as an essential part of that service, the means of actually building the Church, as of testifying that it is built, upon " the foundation of the Apostles and Prophets, Jesus Christ being the head corner-stone." For the worship of the Church in the Eucharistic Anaphora is the fulfilment both of the whole prophetic system of the Old Testament as well as of the Apostolic and Evangelic teaching of the New, and must be shewn to be so. And if in that worship itself the members of the Church are truly "builded together for an habitation of God by the Spirit," it is because they are no more "strangers to the covenants of promise or aliens to the commonwealth of Israel," but "fellow-citizens with the Saints" of the Old Dispensation as of the New, and "of the household of God," the true Israel of God in Christ, and they are this, only as they are built upon the foundation of Apostolic and Prophetic teaching, the teaching of both Old and New Testament.

We may say then that it is only in connection with Eucharistic worship that the Scriptures are truly read and the Psalms truly used. They are then read and used not for mere historical-parænetic purposes, but as bearing witness to their own objective fulfilment in connection with the Eucharistic service, an objective act of faith, as it were, in that Divine Messiahship which Jesus thereby exercises in His Church on earth.

It is sometimes said that only the Temple, not the Synagogue is continued in the Church of Christ. It would be truer to say that in its earthly aspect the Church is the true continuation of the Synagogue, as only in its heavenly aspect is it the true fulfilment of the Temple. It is altogether a mistake to claim for the Church on earth simply as such, or by itself, the prerogatives of the Church in Heaven. The Church on earth is never by itself the true realization of the Communion of Saints, as little is it by itself the true fulfilment of the Temple on Mount Sion. Catholic writers are always afraid, lest by acknowledging this, they should seem to detract from the prerogatives of the Church on earth, or give occasion to Protestants to do so. It is the same mistake which is made in preferring to claim for the Church the power of a new earthly offering of Christ's Body and Blood instead of asserting her participation in Christ's own heavenly offering.

The true prerogative of the Church on earth is her union or capacity of union with the Church in Heaven, such as the Eucharistic service implies, and her consequent participation in the heavenly offering of Christ's Body and Blood. The mistake of Protestantism lies in making the union of the Church on earth with Christ and His Church in Heaven purely subjective, and in denying therefore that objective union which has been constituted by Christ Himself by His appointment of the Eucharistic service. There is no need then for polemical purposes to deny that the Church in her earthly aspect is the true continuation of the Synagogue, and that her Eucharistic worship is in the first instance, only the higher consecration of the worship of the Synagogue. The Synagogue was as much ordained by God as the Temple was. Its worship was as truly divinely appointed, since it was originally inspired by the same Spirit as afterward in fuller measure inspired the worship of the Church. The Synagogue was divinely appointed to be the precursor of the Christian Church, and the Eucharistic worship of the Church, so far as its outward aspect is concerned, has simply grown out of the amalgamation of the worship of the Synagogue with the domestic worship in connection with the observance of the passover. If the Synagogue

F

worship itself is fulfilled in the Eucharistic lections and psalms, and also no doubt in the prayers of the Eucharistic intercession, the Anaphora itself is mainly based, not on any specific form of Temple service, but on the domestic worship of the Passover. As however the observance of the Passover was the link of connection between the worship of the Synagogue and Temple, so the observance of Christ's Eucharistic institution is what specially unites the worship of the Church on earth with the worship of the Church in Heaven, which latter alone is the true fulfilment of the Temple worship. It is this immediate union with the heavenly worship that makes the worship of the Church the true fulfilment and higher consecration of the worship of the Synagogue.

It is a mistake then to regard even the synagogue worship as truly fulfilled except in the Eucharistic lections, psalms, and prayers. The synagogue worship is not fulfilled, as is sometimes thought, in other services of Scripture lections, psalms, and prayers by themselves, and apart from the Eucharistic celebration. The Christian Church is not the true synagogue, the continuation of the synagogue, except as it is the fulfilment of the synagogue in the Eucharistic celebration. If the knowledge of the law and the prophets was sufficient for the Jew, it is the knowledge of their fulfilment that is necessary for the Christian. And therefore the Eucharistic lections, psalms, and prayers have and should be regarded as having, an objective value and significance, which other services of lections, psalms, and prayers by themselves have not.

It is matter for regret, therefore, that the growth of

the private monastic services for the purpose of subjective devotion, mainly consisting, as they do, of psalm and lection, should have had the effect, in the Western Church more especially, of seriously curtailing, and even practically suppressing, the proper Eucharistic use of psalm and lection. While in the East there has been the tendency to mere accumulation of offices of Divine Service, and the lengthening out of such offices, till the whole liturgical system has become utterly unwieldy and unpractical, in the West it has been customary to make up for additions in one direction by curtailments in another. The Eucharistic service has suffered grievously in both ways, both by altogether unnecessary additions and by excessive and unjustifiable curtailment. The public service of the Eucharist has been ruthlessly sacrificed to the exigencies of unnecessarily protracted services of monastic devotion, and to the superfluous punctiliousness of mere personal or official ritual as distinct from the proper ritual of the Eucharist itself. So it has come about that in the present Roman use the Introit, Gradual, Offertory, and Communion Psalms have been reduced for the most part to little more than the saying of a single verse, and even, so far as the service of the people is concerned, practically suppressed, while even the readings from Epistles and Gospels have, as a general rule, been far too much curtailed, and the Old Testament prophecy has only been retained on rare occasions.

And thus, what with the secret recitation of the Canon and the wholesale curtailment of Eucharistic psalm and lection, the present service of the Latin Mass is only the wreck of a former more magnificent and correct liturgical system. It is the Latin Church that has begun that degradation of the Eucharistic service which has only been continued or followed out to its logical consequences in later Anglicanism and Protestantism. If Anglicanism has practically sacrificed the public celebration of the Eucharist to the saying of Morning and Evening prayer, it is the Roman Church itself that has prepared the way by practically sacrificing so much of the service of the Mass to the so-called Canonical offices, which Roman authorities themselves have always represented as the true *Opus Dei*, the true *officium divinum*. And if the Roman Church, while elevating the canonical offices to be apparently the only true rational and spiritual service and worship of God, has at the same time degraded the service of the Mass by the curtailment and practical suppression of the rational and spiritual in it, and by representing its whole meaning and purpose as summed up in the offering of the Body and Blood of Christ by the priest apart from any rational or spiritual co-operation of the people, that is, the Church, is there any wonder that Protestantism should prefer the rational and spiritual service of psalm, lesson, and prayer, to the irrational and unspiritual offering of the Body and Blood of Christ in the Mass? For even if the Mass were that offering of the Body and Blood of Christ which Roman authorities claim it to be, it does not thereby become a rational and spiritual offering.

It is, in fact, the chief ground for condemnation of the Roman theory that it substitutes for the rational and spiritual offering of the sacrifice of Christ in Heaven by the Church on earth, the irrational and unspiritual offering of a new physical, sacramental Body of Christ on earth, and for the rational spiritual worship of God by Christ, and of Christ Himself our High Priest in Heaven, the irrational, unspiritual worship of a new sacramental Christ. And even apart from Roman theory as to the nature of the offering, to make the offering itself a matter of mere dumb show of ritual, so far as the people are concerned, is to make it wholly irrational and unspiritual.

There is then not only sufficient excuse, but ample justification for the Protestant contention that the present Roman service of the Mass is not the true and proper service and worship of God, not the true and proper service of the Christian Eucharist. At the same time, it is to be recognized that this is not the fault so much of the Mass itself in its original form and meaning, or of the liturgical system on which the service was originally based, as of the later Roman theory and practice, which have totally disorganized the service in its liturgical structure and significance, and reduced the greater part of it to a mere external form without inward life and meaning, sacrificing everything to the idea of a mere physical offering of the Body and Blood of Christ by the utterance of the words of consecration. Naturally, if the sacrifice of the Mass consist only in the utterance of the words of consecration, everything else is practically superfluous, and if retained, is only retained for ornament or for form's sake, but not as anywise necessary to the sacrifice of the Church. But the whole Eucharistic service is the true sacrifice of the Church, and not the mere utterance of the words of consecration; and the sacrifice of the Church is not the mere offering of Christ's Body and Blood by the priest for the Church, but the Church's offering of herself to Christ and to God through Christ. The priest is the medium of the Church's offering of herself to Christ, not of the offering of Christ's Body and Blood to God. For he offers the Body and Blood of Christ no otherwise than as the Church offers with him. It is the greatest mistake, and has only led to the degradation and superstitious abuse of the Eucharistic service, to represent the whole sacrifice in it as consisting in the priest's offering of Christ's Body and Blood for the people, and to regard the whole service as only subsidiary to the incidental worship of the sacramental Christ, and not as being itself as a service the means of the true worship of God through Christ.

But though there is thus ample justification for the Protestant rejection and condemnation of the Roman theory and practice of the Mass, this Roman degradation and practical suppression of true Eucharistic service and worship may have been the occasion, but is no justification for the Protestant degradation and suppression of it after another fashion.

One need not hesitate to maintain that the Reformers of the sixteenth century went altogether on the wrong tack in their endeavours to reform the service of the. Church. While their negative attitude towards Roman theory and practice was fully justified, their positive attitude on the whole question of Divine service and worship was open to serious objection. In reaction from the falsely objective Roman worship, they took refuge in forms and ideas of worship more or less purely subjective. In antagonism to the Roman worship of a sacramental Christ, they preferred to regard the Eucharistic service as only for the purpose of subjective sacramental communion, and not for any purpose of objective worship apart from individual communion, for worship only so far as communion is worship.

Now it is true that ancient liturgical precedent may successfully be pleaded against what is called in modern parlance merely "non-communicating attendance," and in favour of an apparent necessity of sacramental participation of all present at the Eucharistic celebration. But can that precedent be truly claimed on behalf of the idea that the whole or the main purpose of the Eucharistic celebration is sacramental participation? It is evident, both from the ancient liturgies and from the very nature of the case, that the main purpose of the Eucharistic celebration as of the sacramental participation itself is worship, the service and worship of Christ and of God through Christ. And if ancient precedent is thought to discountenance so-called "non-communicating attendance," it discountenances still more the idea of any other service but the Eucharistic celebration being the true Christian service and worship of God. To adhere to ancient precedent, we must not provide other so-called services for Christian people to be used as substitutes for the Eucharistic. It is, however, only reasonable to think that the public celebration of Christ's Eucharistic institution may be to the glory of God and of Christ, where the individual sacramental participation of all present might not be.

And we are surely called upon to shew forth the praises of Christ our Redeemer in the Eucharistic commemoration and celebration of His redemption, and to join with the whole Church of Christ in Heaven and earth in the Eucharistic intercession, even when we are not in a position to enjoy the full blessing of the sacramental participation. The real communion of all the faithful by means of sacramental participation is indeed the crown of a true Eucharistic worship, but does not constitute its substance. Rather, it is the true participation in the Church's Eucharistic worship as such that constitutes the substance of a true participation of the Body and Blood of Christ by sacramental communion. Habitual Eucharistic worship is the true preparation for a true sacramental communion. And if the early Church habitually united sacramental communion with Eucharistic worship, it was because Eucharistic worship was the very substance of their spiritual life.

But without a more or less regular and sustained participation in the Eucharistic worship of the Church as such even apart from the idea of individual communion, we are never in a position to enjoy the full blessing of the sacramental communion. And to make the whole purpose of the Eucharistic celebration centre in an individual communion is to degrade the idea of communion itself as well as to lose the true idea of Eucharistic worship. It is as mistaken a view of the Eucharistic consecration to regard it as only for the purpose of the production of the Body and Blood of Christ for individual communion, as it is to regard it as also for the purpose of the production of that Body and Blood in a new form for a new sacramental worship. The mistake is the same in both cases, and consists in regarding the mere utterance of the words of consecration as the immediate production of the Body and Blood of Christ.

It is the whole Eucharistic worship of the Church, as expressed in the ancient forms of Anaphora, of which the utterance of the words of consecration is merely a part, which, as it is the means of enabling the Church on earth to rise to a true participation of the worship of Christ in Heaven, and of God through the sacrifice of Christ as it is present before God in Heaven, is also the means of a true partaking of that sacrifice. If Christ's Body and Blood are in a certain sense "produced" in connection with the sacrament, it is, indeed, truer to say that they are so produced for the purpose of communion than for any purpose of sacramental worship apart from communion. They have no need to be "produced" in the sacrament in order to be worshipped, for they are rather to be worshipped as they are in Heaven in order to be truly "produced" for us for the purpose of a true communion. And if they are thus "produced" for the purpose of a true communion, it is not by the mere utterance of the words of consecration they are produced, but by the whole worship of the Church as it is implied in the Eucharistic Anaphora. This indeed is the justification of the Eastern doctrine, that the Eucharistic consecration is only effected by the invocation of the Holy Ghost. It is, however, as little effected by the mere formal invocation of the Holy Ghost as by the mere formal utterance of the words of institution; it is effected by the whole worship of the Church in the Eucharistic Anaphora as including both. That whole worship is the true invocation of the Holy Ghost, of which the formal invocation is only the more definite expression.

The Protestant idea of the Eucharistic service, or for communion only, is as faulty and inconsistent with true liturgical tradition, as the Roman idea of Eucharistic worship as the worship of a sacramental Christ. Both represent that to be the essential idea of Eucharistic service or worship which in any case can only be the result of Eucharistic service and worship proper. Both reduce the Eucharistic service and worship proper to a minimum, the utterance or remembrance of the words of Institution. They conceive the whole Eucharistic consecration as effected by that and by nothing else. There is no essential difference in principle between the Roman idea of consecration by mere priestly utterance and the Protestant idea of a sufficient consecration by mere subjective remembrance. In the Roman idea there is the real root of all Protestant subjectivism. It is only by a false appearance of objectivism that Roman doctrine conceals its essential subjectivism. The assertion and belief of a new objective presence of Christ on earth by the priestly utterance of the words of institution, do not constitute the true objective presence, which is the presence of Christ in Heaven. And if Roman doctrine creates an object of worship on earth, it does not produce the true object of Holy Communion, which is the sacrifice of Christ as it is offered and accepted for us before God in Heaven. The true objective character of the presence as of the communion, can only be maintained by the assertion of the true objective character of the whole worship of the Eucharistic Anaphora as the means whereby the minds and hearts of the faithful are lifted up to the presence and participation of the sacrifice of Christ upon the heavenly altar.

It was, therefore, an entire mistake on the part of the Reformers of the sixteenth century, English as well as foreign, merely to follow the lead of a vicious Roman practice in the practical suppression of the Eucharistic Anaphora, all but the recitation or memorial utterance of the Words of Institution. This was not to correct sufficiently the Roman abuse of the secret recitation of the whole Canon of the Mass, it was partly to perpetuate the same abuse in another form. The true reform would have been the restoration of something like a proper and complete Eucharistic worship on the lines of the Roman Canon of the Mass or some other ancient liturgy. It might have sufficed that the Canon of the Mass itself should simply be restored to its original use and purpose as the means of the public Eucharistic offering and intercession of the whole Church, and not of the priest alone.

As little was it expedient to follow the Roman lead in the substitution of the Breviary use of psalms and Scripture lessons for the original, more edifying Eucharistic use, whereby it came about that a new subjective worship was established first alongside of, and then practically in lieu of, the true objective Eucharistic. It was natural that at a time when there was a real " famine of hearing the words of the Lord," the slender use of Scripture in the ordinary service of the Mass, in the form for the most part of very short passages from the Epistles and Gospels, should provoke animadversion, as well as the fact that there was no endeavour to make even that little reading intelligible or profitable, while the whole purpose of the Mass was supposed to consist in the alleged re-offering of Christ's Body and Blood by the priest alone, and not in any specific offering of the Church herself to Christ. Much may be said in favour of the retention of a special liturgical language, but it would always have been possible without any sacrifice of principle in that respect, to have read the Eucharistic Scriptures in the vernacular as well as in the liturgical language, after the fashion of the Coptic Church or in accordance with the still earlier practice of the Jewish targumists. However that may be, our English reformers, adhering to the Latin system of short Epistle and Gospel in the Eucharistic service, took advantage of the fact of there being also a certain system of Old Testament lections in the Breviary office of Mattins, to reduce and popularize the more important of the Breviary offices by grafting on to the orderly recitation of the Psalter a more extended system of lections both from the Old and New Testaments. It may be doubted whether this new departure in liturgical worship, however honest an endeavour to meet a great want of the time, was an unmixed gain. Anglican

Mattins even with the Eucharistic service superadded is as little the ideal of the worship of the Christian Church as the Roman Mass.

Moreover, as experience has shewn, the Anglican system, because it has been so long coupled with the Protestant idea of the Eucharist as for communion only, has led to the practical dethronement of the Eucharistic service, and to the suppression of the very idea of Eucharistic worship as the true worship of the Christian Church. So far as the use of the Psalter is concerned, it can only be characterized as a grave liturgical mistake to extrude the Psalms altogether from the Eucharistic service, in order only to heap them up elsewhere for a more or less mechanical recitation of them in their accidental numerical order. This mechanical recitation of the Psalms in their numerical order, whether after the arrangement of the Latin Breviary or the English Book of Common Prayer, is no sufficient compensation for the loss of the original Eucharistic use and application of the Psalms, of which traces still remain in the Missal.

The Eucharistic application of the Psalms is of far greater importance to us than the mere frequent recitation of them, and it is just for want of this definite application of them that their real meaning to us is so often lost, so that it is taken for granted that it is only for their general religous tone and in the purely deistic or Jewish sense of them that we use them in our Christian worship. As to the lessons, while it would have been an undoubted advantage to have restored the Old Testament lessons to their proper place in the Eucharistic service, corresponding to the Lectio prophetica of the Gallican and Mozarabic liturgies, and also of some parts of the Roman Missal, and even to have extended the Old Testament lessons into the double form of "the Law and the Prophets," corresponding to the New Testament Epistle and Gospel, on the other hand the Anglican system of New Testament lessons at Mattins and Evensong only causes unnecessary confusion and interference with the Eucharistic Epistle and Gospel, the liturgical importance of which latter is thereby considerably depressed. It would have been more consonant with liturgical propriety to have improved and extended the system of Eucharistic Epistles and Gospels, all the more that it seems as if those still remaining in the English service had often been unnecessarily curtailed in the older service whence they were taken. The suppression and curtailment of Eucharistic lections, like the practical suppression and curtailment of the Canon itself, was one of the very points in which the later Latin service stood in most urgent need of correction and reform.

These curtailments were partly the result, partly also the cause, of the growth of the idea that the sole object of the saying of Mass was the offering of the Body and Blood of Christ by the priest alone. It was not the true path of liturgical reform to leave these curtailments in the Eucharistic service just as they were, and at the same time to substitute other services with fuller Scripture lections to take the place of a virtually effete Eucharistic service; effete, that is, for the general purpose of Christian worship. A mechanical distribution of Epistles and

Gospels, like the mechanical distribution of the Psalter, without any regard to liturgical appropriateness, was no proper substitute for an improved and enlarged scheme of Eucharistic lections, fitting more or less into each other with the help of appropriate Psalms and Canticles, and always pointing to their true fulfilment in connection with Eucharistic worship itself.

Incidentally it may be pointed out, that in the Anglican service a too servile following of the order in the Breviary has resulted in a very unsuitable arrangement of the Canticles in connection with the Lessons. It is surely more fitting that the Benedictus follow the lesson from the Old Testament, and the Te Deum and Magnificat the Lesson from the New, rather than *vice versâ*. What is the Te Deum itself, but, like the Laudamus of the Gloria in Excelcis, a reminiscence of some early form of Eucharistic Anaphora? This only helps to emphasize the fact that it is only in connection with Eucharistic worship, and as a real part of the Eucharistic service, that either Canticles or Lessons have their true meaning, that is, their true spiritual meaning for us as members of the Church of Christ, as distinct from their general religious historical meaning.

It may be thought that the Canonical offices of Psalms and Lections have a sufficient general connection with the Eucharistic service, by reason of their being only a part of the general worship of the Church as the Eucharistic service itself. But as has been argued above, this is no sufficient justification for the extrusion of these important elements of worship from the Eucharistic service itself, besides that it has given rise to the erroneous ideas of the independence and self-sufficiency of these other forms of worship, and that the Eucharistic service as such, whether with or without communion, is only a small part of the worship of the Church, and not her real, whole, and true worship.

And let it be understood here that by Eucharistic worship is properly meant not the mere worship of a sacramental Christ, produced by the utterance of the words of consecration after the Roman idea, but the whole true worship of God through Christ as the High Priest of the Christian profession, acting as such by His perpetual offering of His sacrifice of the Cross for us before God in Heaven, and realized to us as such by means of the Eucharistic service. It is not to be allowed, therefore, that other services may be in themselves the true Christian worship of God as such, while the Eucharistic service is only for the special worship of Christ in His sacramental presence or in His sacramental gift of Himself. The Christian, that is, the true worship of God, cannot be separated from the worship of Christ, and the true worship of Christ cannot be separated from the true worship of God by Him, that is, our worship of God through His worship in the perpetual offering of His sacrifice of the Cross. Christ not only said, "I ascend to My Father and your Father," but also, "to My God and your God." The true God, the God of Christian worship, is the God and Father of our Lord Jesus Christ.

Our worship of Christ then is not something over and above our worship of God, but there is no other true worship of God, but that which is through the sacrifice of Christ as Christ Himself has enabled His Church to take part with Him in His perpetual offering of it before God in Heaven. It is a mistake therefore to regard, whether after the Roman or Protestant fashion, the ordinary Canonical offices, or offices of psalm, lection, prayer only as specially the worship of God, and the Eucharistic service as specially the worship of Christ whether in His sacramental presence or in His sacramental gift. It is Romanism that has introduced this false dualism into Christian worship. It has reduced Eucharistic worship to the worship of the sacramental Christ only. And even if it represents this worship to be also the worship of God, yet it is not properly the worship of God by Christ, but is only improperly termed the worship of God, because it is the worship of Christ. Or if the worship of God is thought to consist in the offering of the Body and Blood of Christ, yet this offering and therefore this worship is the act of the priest alone or of Christ through the priest; it may be the worship of God for the people, but it is not the worship of God by the people.

As the rôle of the priest is thought to consist in the making present and the consequent offering of the sacramental Christ, so the rôle of the people is made to consist in the worship of the sacramental Christ thus made present and offered for them. Romanism having thus abused and misrepresented Eucharistic worship by reducing it to the worship of the sacramental Christ, is there any wonder that Protestantism should think to restore the worship of God altogether apart from a

Eucharistic worship so discredited? Anglicanism more especially could appeal in self-justification to the Roman conception of the canonical offices as the true *officium divinum*. If the Canonical offices were the *officium divinum*, the true worship of God for the monastic orders and the clergy, there was no reason why they should not be reduced to a more practical form in order to be the *officium divinum*, or the true worship of God for the laity. Better this, certainly, than that the laity should be thought to be necessarily excluded from the direct worship of God, and have to content themselves with the mere worship of the sacramental Christ in lieu of the worship of God, or with the still lower and more mistaken worship of Mary and Saints after the Roman fashion.

Romanism itself justifies the view of the Canonical offices, or offices on the same model, as the true and proper worship of God, while it has also given occasion and sufficient excuse for the Protestant rejection of Eucharistic worship as of the doctrine of the Communion of Saints. A rationalistic subjective Protestantism has only developed the rationalistic subjective element in Romanism. The mistake of Protestantism with regard to the worship of God is as great a mistake on the other side, and yet fundamentally the same kind of mistake, as the Roman worship of the sacramental Christ and the Communion of Saints. The Romanist worship of the sacramental Christ and of the Saints is as purely rationalist subjective as the Protestant worship of God, as little the true objective worship of Christ and the Communion of Saints as it is the true objective worship of God.

It is as great a mistake to falsify Eucharistic worship as to reject it. Romanism has falsified it, Protestantism rejects it more or less, it rejects it so far as it considers the worship of God to be complete or sufficient without it. But however the falsification may have furnished excuse for this rejection it does not wholly justify it. The worship of God which virtually claims to be independent of the Eucharistic service of God and of Christ is not the true Christian worship of God, because it is not the worship of God by Christ by the sacrifice of Christ. The worship of God through Christ or in the name of Christ is not a worship with the mere mention of the name of Christ or the bare mental remembrance of Christ, but it is the worship of God by the offering with Christ of His own very sacrifice, as He has enjoined this offering upon us.

There is no room therefore for such a distinction as is often drawn, as well in Anglican theory as in Anglican practice, of a higher and a lower worship of God, the lower worship, the ordinary worship of the ordinary Christian, as provided in the ordinary offices of Mattins and Evensong, the higher worship, the special worship of the sincere communicant Christian in the service of Holy Communion. It might be urged, indeed, that so far as the language of worship is concerned, our English Mattins and Evensong presume the worship of the communicant Christian, not the worship of the non-communicant. The language of the Psalms and Canticles, as language of worship, is only true in the mouth of communicant Christians, not non-communicants. And therefore if it be desirable to have a Missa Catechumenorum for ordinary Christians, the unfaithful "faithful," as distinct from the Missa Fidelium for the true "faithful," such service should not be precisely on the model of our English Mattins and Evensong, but pitched in a somewhat lower key, a service of instruction and prayer, but not of Christian praise in the jubilant tone of the Canticles Te Deum and Magnificat. These Canticles belong essentially to the Church's sacrifice of praise, which none are qualified to offer but those who are in full communion with the Church.

So far then from its being true to say that Mattins and Evensong are the proper form of service for the ordinary Mass of non-communicant nominal Christians, it would be truer to say they are only appropriate for the use of sincere, habitual communicant members of the Church. And it is far more in accordance with what we know to be the origin of the Canonical offices to regard them as a certain prolongation of the Eucharistic worship of the Church, rather than as ever intended to be a separate, independent worship of God, to be used as a sufficient ordinary substitute for a proper Eucharistic worship by those who are either indisposed or disqualified to take part in that worship. The Canonical office might also legitimately be conceived as a certain preparation for Eucharistic worship, but not as a remote preparation subjectively for an occasional Eucharistic celebration and Sacramental participation, but as the immediate objective preparation of that Eucharistic worship of which they only form a part. It is only as they are a preparation in this latter sense that the invitatory Psalm Venite has its true meaning.

But whether the Canonical offices be conceived as a preparation or prolongation of Eucharistic worship, it was a misfortune for the worship of the Church generally that their over-luxuriant development brought about, in the West more especially, the deterioration and impoverishment of the proper Eucharistic service and worship. And, strangely enough, while they have thus brought about the deterioration and impoverishment of the proper Eucharistic service, they have also themselves ceased, for the most part, to be any real part of the public worship of the Latin Church.

It follows, however, that even as retained in their reduced more practical forms of English Mattins and Evensong, these offices or services have no real *raison d'être* as worship or Christian worship apart from Eucharistic worship, and they should not therefore be conceived as being in themselves that true worship of God which they are not. Conceived as a separate independent worship of God, they are not the true worship, because they are not distinctively Christian worship. The mere use of Christian language does not constitute distinctively Christian worship. Words of praise and prayer are indeed an essential part of the Church's sacrifice of praise and prayer, but they do not constitute the whole of that sacrifice. In order to be true Christian praise and prayer, they must be united with the great act of praise and prayer which is implied in the Eucharistic commemoration of the sacrifice of

Christ, and in the union by that commemoration of the interceding Church on earth with the interceding Church in Heaven and with the intercessory work of Christ Himself in Heaven. Christian praise must be the definitely Eucharistic praise associated with the Eucharistic celebration, as Christian prayer must also be the prayer which is taken up into the Eucharistic intercession. It is only so that praise is truly worthy of God and prayer effectual. It is the Eucharistic celebration that makes both praise and prayer worthy and effectual. The Eucharistic celebration is not just necessary in order to sacramental reception, but for the due offering of the Church's sacrifice of praise and prayer. As little as the Eucharistic acts of consecration are to be dissociated from the Church's words of praise and prayer, as little is the Church's offering of praise and prayer to be dissociated from the Eucharistic acts.

It is the Roman Church that has first dissociated the Eucharistic act or acts of consecration from the Eucharistic words which constitute the Church's sacrifice of praise and prayer. For the Eucharistic words are not the mere words of consecration so-called, but the words of praise and prayer of the Church in which Christ's words of institution are embedded. The Roman Church has dissociated the Eucharistic acts from the Eucharistic words by representing the whole sacrifice as consisting in the utterance, by the priest alone, of Christ's words of institution, and thus regarding the Eucharistic prayers and praises of the Church as constituting no part of the offering of the Body and Blood of Christ.

As Romanism has dissociated the Eucharistic acts from the Eucharistic words, so Protestantism the Eucharistic words from the Eucharistic acts. By a natural reaction from the Romish view, Protestantism has regarded the mere words of praise and prayer, even apart from any Eucharistic celebration, to be the Church's sacrifice of praise and prayer, and that celebration itself as only for the purpose of sacramental reception. But this dissociation of Eucharistic words from Eucharistic acts is as mistaken as the Roman dissociation of Eucharistic acts from the Eucharistic words. For this separation of ordinary worship from the properly Eucharistic, combined with the resolution of this latter into mere sacramental reception, is the practical reduction of Christian theology, as of Christian worship, to Socinianism on the one hand and Zwinglianism on the other.

These forms of heresy only draw the legitimate conclusions from an imperfect or mistaken practice of Christian worship. For Christian theology is essentially practical, and a dry orthodoxy can never successfully resist the assaults of heresy. Christian theology and Christian worship are inextricably bound up together, so that a true theology can only be upheld by a true worship. God is only the object of our belief because He is the object of our worship. We believe in God as the Being to be worshipped, and we only truly believe in the God Whom we truly worship.

As has been already indicated, it is only Eucharistic worship, by which we mean not the Roman production and worship of a sacramental Christ, but the real, direct worship of God and of Christ by the Church on earth in union with the Church in Heaven by means of the public celebration of Christ's Eucharistic Institution, which is the true confession of faith in all the great truths of the Christian revelation, the true confession of Christian Faith in the Divine Trinity, the Incarnation of the Eternal Word, the Atonement wrought by the Sacrifice of Christ, the reality and perfection of the grace of Christ's Sacraments and the glory of the Communion of Saints.

We truly believe in the Divine Trinity, not when we simply acknowledge the threefold personality God the Father, Son, and Holy Ghost, but when we worship God the Father by worshipping through the Only-Begotten Son made man for us, and in the Holy Ghost, the Spirit of the Son, proceeding from the Father, but sent forth to us from the Incarnate Son to enable us thus to worship the Father in Spirit and in truth in the faithful observance of the Eucharistic Institution of Christ.

We only believe in the Incarnate Son and truly acknowledge Christ as God, when worshipping God through Him, we also worship Christ Himself in His glorified manhood as our Divine Mediator, the High Priest of our Christian profession. We only truly worship Christ as God when we worship God through Him as Man by the means for the purpose which He as Man has ordained. We only truly believe in the Atonement which Christ has wrought by the sacrifice of the Cross when by the Eucharist we acknowledge the perpetuity of Christ's High-Priestly offering of it for us before God in Heaven.

We only truly believe in the full reality of the grace of

the sacraments, the full reality of the divine redemption and Christian sanctification, the sanctification of the Spirit, when we acknowledge that it is the very purpose of Holy Baptism to make us kings and priests to God in the offering of the Eucharistic sacrifice, that is, so to sprinkle our hearts from an evil conscience that we have boldness to enter into the holiest by the Blood of Jesus, both to take part with Him in the offering of the eternal sacrifice, and to partake of the sacrifice there offered as He presents it to us for the purpose and enables us so to do.

We only truly believe in the Communion of Saints as we acknowledge that by the Eucharistic celebration the Church on earth is united with the Church in Heaven in the common worship of God and of the Lamb. Eucharistic worship then, in the sense here indicated as the Church's public worship of God through Christ in the perpetual offering of His Atoning Sacrifice, is the practical confession of faith in all the great mysteries of the Christian religion, apart from which these mysteries have no real meaning for us. It is the true worship of God, Father, Son, and Holy Ghost, the true worship of Christ as God and of Christ the God-Man in His Atoning Sacrifice, the true worship of the Communion of Saints. Apart from Eucharistic worship, professedly Christian worship sinks to the level of practical Socinianism and Zwinglianism; it may be the worship of God the Creator, the God of nature and natural providence, but it is not the sufficient worship of God the Redeemer and Sanctifier, the God of all grace and truth.

But if Protestantism is so far guilty of a rejection or suppression of distinctively Christian worship by its rejection or suppression of Eucharistic worship, Romanism is more guilty; it has both led the way in the separation of ordinary worship from Eucharistic, and has given occasion to the Protestant rejection of Eucharistic worship by its falsification of the nature of that worship. The Roman worship of the Mass is not true Eucharistic worship. It is not the Canon of the Mass that is at fault, but Roman theory and practice are not the true theory and practice of Eucharistic worship, to which the Canon bears witness. The Roman worship is not true Eucharistic worship, because it is not the true worship of Christ, nor the true worship of God by Christ. It is not the true worship of Christ, because it is not the true immediate worship of the heavenly Christ, Christ in His heavenly glory acting as our great High Priest in the perpetual offering of His one efficacious sacrifice.

The worship of a sacramental Christ is not the worship of the heavenly Christ, for on Roman theory the sacramental Christ is not the mere presence of the heavenly Christ, that is, His heavenly presence made present to us on earth by means of the Sacrament, but it is a new earthly presence of Christ, distinct altogether from His true heavenly presence.

As little as the Roman worship is the true worship of Christ, as little is it the true worship of God by Christ. It is not Christ's true worship of God, since it is not the offering of that one sacrifice by which Christ perfected man's worship of God. It is not the Church's true worship of God by Christ, since the offering of the Body and Blood of Christ is held to be by the priest alone for the Church, not directly by the Church with the priest, or, as it should more truly be said, by the priest only with and through the Church. The offering of the Body and Blood of Christ is indeed the true worship of God by Christ, but the only true offering of that Body and Blood by the Church is the participation in Christ's heavenly act of offering, and for this reason the utterance of the words of consecration is not the direct offering of the Body and Blood of Christ, but only the means to the participation in the heavenly act of offering, and the priest has no more direct participation in that act of offering than the whole Church has.

Nor is the utterance of the words of consecration even the whole means to the participation in the heavenly offering, but it is that means only as it is part of the whole Eucharistic prayer by which the Church is spiritually enabled to offer aright the Body and Blood of Christ in union with Christ's own intercessory offering, to offer them therefore to those ends and for those purposes for which Christ Himself offers them and desires them to be offered. The offering of the Body and Blood of Christ is not a mere physical act but a spiritual act. It was only through the Eternal Spirit Christ first offered Himself, as through the same Eternal Spirit He continues to offer the same sacrifice He once offered, though now with all its own glorious results in Himself and therefore in its glorious perfection, and it is only through the same Spirit the Church on earth can join with Him in offering that sacrifice, and that Spirit is His own Spirit of supplication and intercession, the Spirit by which in the days of His flesh He offered up prayers and supplications to God in the offering of the sacrifice of the Cross, and by which He now ever liveth to make intercession for us.

It is only this spirit of supplication and intercession that enables the Church to offer aright the sacrifice of Christ's Body and Blood; to offer aright, that is, to offer spiritually, and not merely physically, for even if the physical offering were possible without the spiritual, yet without the spiritual it is absolutely null and void. The spiritual offering is indeed so far dependent upon physical acts, but does not simply consist in these physical acts, and therefore the spiritual offering of the Body and Blood of Christ does not consist in the mere physical utterance by the priest of the words of consecration so-called, but in the supplications and intercessions of the Church on the ground of that utterance, and offered by the priest only as the mouthpiece of the Church.

To sum up, then, the Roman worship of the Mass is both in its theory and practice a falsification of that original Eucharistic worship of the Church, the theory and practice of which is sufficiently attested by all ancient liturgies, the Canon of the Mass itself included. The Roman worship of the Mass in its present form is as little the true Christian worship of God and of Christ as ordinary Protestant non-Eucharistic worship is. While, therefore, one may be fully sensible of the serious declension of Protestant and ordinary Anglican worship from the primitive standard of Eucharistic worship, one has also to remember that this very declension is due as well in its negative as in its positive aspect to Romanism; in its negative aspect as a rejection or suppression of Eucharistic worship by a natural reaction from Roman falsification, in its positive aspect as the substitution of an inferior kind of worship, by direct derivation from the Roman Church of the theory and practice of a purely subjective worship.

One may be fully sensible of the serious defects of Protestant and Anglican worship, and yet recognize it to be an utter mistake to think to restore a proper Eucharistic worship in the Anglican Communion by the mere adoption or revival of the leading ideas of Roman or Western mediæval theory and practice of the Mass. Rome equally with ourselves has lost the true tradition of Eucharistic worship. She has preserved more of the dead form of it, but it is she who has emptied her own form of worship of real life, both for herself and for us. As has been pointed out, the very defects of the Anglican service, as of Protestant worship generally, are derived from Romanism. Protestantism has only developed in a truer form the inherent subjectivism of Western mediævalism. It has substituted the subjective worship of God for the subjective worship of the sacramental presence, or of Mary and the Saints.

How has it come about that the English Church has reduced the Eucharistic Anaphora to the so-called Prayer of Consecration, the memorial utterance of the words of institution? It is only because the Latin Church had by the secret recitation of the Canon practically reduced it to nothing but the utterance of these words, regarding everything else in the Canon as virtually of no account. How comes it that the English Church has so largely developed other services like Mattins and Evensong at the expense of a proper Eucharistic service? It is only because the Latin Church has already done the same thing in another way. It is the Latin Church that has been guilty of this double mutilation of the Eucharistic service, which rendered the appointment of other services for the people's worship of God really necessary. And to what end this double mutilation, but to make the frequent saying of Mass by the priest alone more easy and convenient, and then to justify the idea that the whole purpose of the saying of the Mass is the alleged offering of the Body and Blood of Christ by the priest alone, and not any offering whatsoever of the faith and devotion of the Church herself? And certainly if the whole purpose of the Eucharistic service is only the offering of Christ's Body and Blood by the priest alone in the utterance of the words of consecration, everything else in the service is of little or no consequence and its retention is only a matter of superfluous form or ceremony.

But a theory of the Eucharistic service which makes everything practically and objectively superfluous except the utterance of Christ's words, is self-condemned, because it creates an unnecessary dualism between the subjective and objective in Christian worship, which hinders their true reconciliation. This dualism is the destruction of all spiritual worship, and is not in accordance with the Eucharistic prayer of any liturgy as little as it is a true interpretation of the words "Do this in remembrance." It is absurd to interpret the words "Do this" as merely meaning "Say this," and if to "do this" is to offer a sacrifice, it is to offer the whole sacrifice of Eucharistic praise and devotion as the Spirit sent from Christ upon His Church inspires and enables the Church to do. It is to think little indeed of the dispensation of the Spirit to the Church to think that nothing else is of any objective consequence in Christian worship but the mechanical utterance of Christ's words by the priest alone.

The Eastern Church is far more in the right when it asserts that the mere utterance of the sacred words effects nothing without the invocation of the Holy Spirit, only the true invocation of the Holy Spirit is not the mere formal invocation by the priest, but that which is implied and contained in the whole Eucharistic service as the offering of the Church's bounden duty of Eucharistic praise and prayer.

In the Eucharistic celebration the priest is only the mouthpiece of the Church, not the mouthpiece of Christ, except so far as Christ or the Spirit of Christ speaks also in His Church. It is His Church, and His ministers as part of His Church, that Christ commands "Do this in remembrance of Me," and the words are "Do this in remembrance," and not "Do this in My person." The priest acts in the person of the remembering Church, not in the person of Christ. It is not Christ Who merely offers through the priest, but Christ requires from His Church some offering of her own, in order that she may take her fitting part in His offering in Heaven. The priest is the medium of the offering of the Church, not the medium of the offering of Christ, except so far as Christ adds to His own offering in Heaven the offering of His Church on earth, but what Christ thus adds to His own offering in Heaven is no other offering of His Body and Blood, but the offering of the thanksgiving praises and prayers of His Church. It is of the utmost importance then that the thanksgiving praises and prayers of the Church be brought into the closest possible connection with the memorial utterance of Christ's words of blessing on the Eucharistic bread and wine, for it is by her own thanksgiving praises and prayers, and not by the mere utterance of certain words, that she is privileged to take part in Christ's heavenly offering of His Body and Blood. The Roman theory of the immediate offering of the Body and Blood of Christ by the priest alone, or by the priest in the person of Christ, by the mere utterance of the words of consecration, apart altogether from the Church's offering of her bounden duty of Eucharistic praise and prayer, is as false as it is unwarranted by any Scriptural or liturgical evidence.

Fully acknowledging then the comparative worthlessness of a non-Eucharistic Christian worship, admitting also the serious defects of ordinary Anglican worship by its neglect and comparative depreciation of the Eucharistic observance, and the faulty structure of the Anglican Communion Service from a liturgical point of view, one must yet recognize it to be an utter mistake to think to restore the true practice of Eucharistic worship in the Church of England by the mere adoption of certain parts of Tridentine Roman theory and practice.

A true practice must rest on a true theory, and this, the endeavour has here been made to shew, the Roman theory is not. Roman theory and practice are as much the falsification and degradation of true Eucharistic worship as Anglican theory and practice has been the mistaken depreciation of it, and Protestant theory and practice its rejection. A true theory of Eucharistic worship must start from the acknowledgment of the identity of the worship of the Church on earth with the worship of the Church in Heaven, an identity secured only by the observance of Christ's Eucharistic institution. And it is to be noted that the observance of Christ's Eucharistic institution does not consist in the mere saying of His words of institution, but in the Church's whole Eucharistic offering of faith and prayer, by which the Spirit of Christ inspires and enables the Church to observe Christ's institution.

By the Eucharistic institution, therefore, and the whole Eucharistic service, the Church, and not the priest only, has boldness to enter into the holiest, is privileged to enter spiritually the immediate presence of God in Heaven, where alone the true sacrifice continues to be offered, as it is there alone that it is truly offered by Him Who is the High Priest for ever after the order of Melchizedek. The Sursum Corda is the key of the Eucharistic service, and is the call to that subjective elevation of heart and mind which is only the inward realization of the truth of that heavenly presence of the

H

heavenly sacrifice as it is objectively manifested by the Holy Spirit by means of Christ's Eucharistic institution.

There is therefore no offering of Christ's Body and Blood but that which takes place in Heaven, and any theory of the Eucharistic presence or the Eucharistic sacrifice which maintains or suggests the contrary is to be rejected as evidently false. It is as false to say that there is an offering on earth which is a repetition of the offering in Heaven, as to say that it is an altogether new offering of Christ's Body and Blood. It is not the purpose of the Eucharistic consecration to bring down Christ from Heaven to earth for a new offering, but it is the purpose of the whole Eucharistic service as such to raise the Church on earth both subjectively and objectively through the power of the Holy Spirit to the heavenly presence of Christ, so as to take part with Christ in His heavenly offering and partake of His sacrifice there offered. The Eucharistic presence is no new presence or new mode of presence on earth, but the heavenly presence itself invisibly but spiritually manifested to the minds and hearts of Christ's faithful in the power of the Holy Spirit proceeding from Christ Himself in Heaven. And this heavenly presence in the Eucharist is no mere subjective presence, but really objective, because the Spirit Who reveals it is the Spirit of Truth proceeding from Christ to glorify Christ to the minds and hearts of His faithful, that "Spirit of Truth Whom the world cannot receive, because it seeth Him not neither knoweth Him."

The Eucharistic mystery is no ridiculous earthly mystery as the Roman theory of transubstantiation represents it, the useless unnecessary disappearance of earthly substances, but a heavenly and spiritual mystery, the very mystery of which consists in the presence of heavenly things with and by means of the earthly things, a heavenly presence spiritually discerned, and not an earthly presence rationally discerned. The Spirit of Truth effects no such conjuring trick as that of transubstantiation, but reveals the glory of the heavenly presence of Christ by means of the earthly things which Christ Himself has appointed for the purpose.

If then we are to endeavour after the restoration of the Eucharistic service to its true place in connection with Christian worship, we must not be misled into adopting any theory of a real presence by the mere utterance of the words of consecration so-called, or of a real offering of Christ's Body and Blood by the priest alone, or by his utterance of the sacred words. The true real presence is Christ's presence in Heaven, to which the Church's whole service of Eucharistic praise and prayer is Christ's appointed means of bringing us near. The true offering of Christ's Body and Blood is Christ's offering in Heaven, in which He calls His whole Church to take part with Him, and not the priest alone, or the priest for the Church. The earthly priest is the appointed medium for the offering of the Church's sacrifice of faith and prayer, not for any direct offering of Christ's Body and Blood, in which indeed the priest can only take part with the Church.

In the Eucharistic service, then, the Church on earth is not called upon simply to attend upon the priest's alleged offering of Christ's Body and Blood, but to bring her own sacrifice of faith and prayer as the means whereby she may take a true part in Christ's perpetual intercessory offering for her. It is the utter degradation of the Church's Eucharistic service to turn it into the mere saying of Mass by the individual priest. It is just this which has led to the suppression of everything that is properly and characteristically Eucharistic in the service, and whatever in it is specially significant of its being the Church's public offering of faith and prayer.

Nor is it enough to constitute it the Church's public offering of faith and prayer that the individual members of the Church unite their private subjective devotions with the private saying of the service by the priest. The whole Eucharistic service should be the Church's public offering of faith and prayer, with the priest as her audible mouthpiece. And all the elements of Christian worship should be united in connection with the Eucharistic celebration, so that the whole interest and value of that celebration, whether for worship or for communion, should not be regarded as concentrated in the mere utterance of the words of consecration so-called. There should be no unnecessary dualism between ordinary and Eucharistic worship, and the completeness of a true Eucharistic service and worship should not be sacrificed to the mere ease and convenience of frequent and multiplied celebrations. There is no particular merit or value in mere multiplied consecrations.

It is this idea that has helped to bring about the mischievous mutilation and unnecessary curtailment of most important parts of the Eucharistic office in the Western Church. There should be as little need to supplement the Church's Eucharistic service of praise and prayer by elaborate Canonical offices as by Marianic and other popular Roman devotions. But as things are, whether in the Roman or the Anglican Church, there is need to supplement the existing mutilated and curtailed Eucharistic office by other offices and devotions, although this only creates an unnatural separation between ordinary and Eucharistic worship, the subjective and the objective, and hinders the Eucharistic service from being the true offering up of the Church's whole sacrifice of praise and prayer.

The true notion of the Eucharistic sacrifice is that which regards it, not as the priest's offering up of Christ's Body and Blood by the utterance only of the words of consecration, but as the Church's whole sacrifice of praise and prayer, of faith and devotion, offered up in union with Christ's own perpetual intercessory offering up of the Sacrifice of the Cross, His Body and Blood, immediately before God in Heaven. It is so, that Christ is truly offered up by the Church "on the sacrifice and service of the Church's faith," and that the Eucharistic bread and wine are truly "sanctified by the Holy Ghost," to be the means of the Church's participation of "all spiritual blessings in heavenly places."

# Postscript

ON

## RIVAL PROGRAMMES IN THE CHURCH OF ENGLAND.

SOME of the comments in the above were partly suggested by the appearance of a book entitled "The Lord's Day and the Holy Eucharist," consisting of a series of essays by various writers of the so-called Catholic school in the Church of England, in which a certain programme is set forth with regard to the more general restoration of Eucharistic worship in our Churches.

With the main idea of this programme the present writer is in the fullest sympathy, with the endeavour, that is, to restore the Eucharistic service to its true place in connection with all Christian worship. As the foregoing remarks, however, will shew, he cannot but think that this idea will never be properly carried out, until a more serious endeavour is made to arrive at a truer appreciation of the Eucharistic service and of Eucharistic worship both dogmatically and liturgically, and until English Churchmen of the so-called Catholic school rise above their too servile dependence on Roman or Latin mediæval ideas with regard to Catholic doctrine and practice.

Even granting the serious defects of ordinary Anglican doctrine and practice, granting that our own table does not provide enough of the good things of the Kingdom of God, are we simply to be content with some further miserable crumbs we can pick up from the Roman table? The Roman Church may appear to provide upon her table of doctrine and practice more of the good things of the Kingdom of God, but she cannot wholly be acquitted of the charge of having so tampered with sacred things, and so mixing poisonous drugs of her own with the things of the Lord, as to have made the table of the Lord contemptible to the Christian, as well as the unbelieving, Protestant world, and even in the eyes of those who have desired to be Catholic Christians. If we are to offer the pure offering and true incense of Christian worship in the fulfilment of our Eucharistic service to Christ and to God through Him, we must recur to a sounder liturgical doctrine and practice than what late mediæval or present Roman theories can furnish us with. It is only so we shall ever succeed in shaking and removing the objections and prejudices of the Christian Protestant world against the restoration of the Eucharistic Service to its true place in any true system of Christian faith and worship, objections and prejudices, which otherwise have only too real a foundation and too legitimate an excuse.

These additional remarks have been called forth by the fact of the writer's attention having been called, since the foregoing "Considerations" were written, to a pamphlet by Archdeacon Sinclair, on " The prospects of the principles of the Reformation in the Church of England," which is also, by way of comment, on the "Lord's Day and the Holy Eucharist," taken as being the "latest manifesto" of the so-called "sacerdotal or mediæval" school in the Church of England, and in which an opposition programme, claiming to be based on "primitive Catholic principles," is suggested for the Protestant evangelical party in the same Church. It is, perhaps, a gratifying "sign of the times" that the Archdeacon should counsel his own party in the Church to shew more outward charity and civility to those whom they regard as their opponents, but little would be gained if this outward charity and civility is only to be the mask for a real bitter inward hostility, without any endeavour to appreciate or enter into the least sympathy with the opposite point of view. Real Christian charity requires of us all more than a merely conventional civility and politeness, and if all that the Archdeacon's advice amounts to is that the Protestant party refrain from outwardly molesting their opponents, we are not very far on the way to a true eirenicon in the Church of England. The Archdeacon himself does not appear to believe such an eirenicon possible, and only hopes to accomplish by spiritual force, what he recognizes as hopeless to accomplish by the brute force of legal prosecution.

However charitably couched then, his pamphlet is really a declaration of war, only the war is henceforth to be waged on more approved modern principles, the battle to be fought with more spiritual weapons than heretofore. But before engaging in this warfare, it is a question to be considered, whether the programme put before us in this pamphlet is any whit more justifiable than the opposite programme. Archdeacon Sinclair assumes that no choice is left to us but between mediæval sacerdotalism, and Protestant evangelicalism in his modified reassertion of it, which he claims to be primitive and Catholic. The foregoing "Considerations" will have been written in vain if they do not shew this at least, that a third way is open, which may be more primitive and Catholic than either of the other two, while it has the further advantage of including both in a higher synthesis, containing every element of truth in either separately, but excluding their respective errors whether by excess or defect.

Archdeacon Sinclair thinks that "the terms High Church and Low Church have nothing whatever to do with the distinctions between" the two opposite parties in the Church of England, and "are altogether misleading." These terms, however, are far more appropriate and less misleading than those which he proposes to substitute in their place. If the Archdeacon rejects them, it is only that he may embrace all honest High-Churchmen under the designation of "mediæval sacerdotalists," and claim for Low-Churchmen as such, and even as they are at the same time Protestant evangelicals, the proud title of "primitive or reformed Catholics."

But it is only to confuse the issues to represent the question as one between mediæval sacerdotalism only on the one hand and Protestant evangelicalism only on the other. There may be a question between mediæval sacerdotalism on the one hand and primitive Catholicity on the other, but even so, there will still remain the further question between primitive Catholicity and Protestant evangelicalism ordinarily so-called, for not only is it a very large assumption simply to identify the two latter on the ground of their supposed common opposition to mediæval sacerdotalism, but with what form of Protestant evangelicalism ordinarily so-called is primitive Catholicity to be identified, since Protestant evangelicalism has many forms, and its Anglican is indeed its least consistent form. But even apart from these further ramifications of the question as to primitive Catholicity, the designations "sacerdotalism" and "evangelicalism" are altogether misleading. Protestant evangelicalism ordinarily so-called has as little right historical or spiritual to arrogate to itself the title "evangelical" as "mediæval sacerdotalism" has to be regarded as a true High Churchism, or a genuine legitimate development of the same. There is a true and a false sacerdotalism as there is a true and a false evangelicalism, and there may be more in common between a true "sacerdotalism" and a true "evangelicalism," than what those who labour to accentuate the opposition between them usually imagine.

To take the question of sacerdotalism first. Latin mediæval and later Roman sacerdotalism is not the true sacerdotalism, because it magnifies the individual priest as such above the Church as such; it denies the priesthood of the Church in order to claim all divine priesthood, even the priesthood of Christ Himself, for the individual earthly priest; it asserts that Christ Himself only now exercises His own priesthood through the earthly priests He has appointed in His place; and because it thus denies Christ's own immediate exercise of His priesthood in Heaven, it denies the priesthood of the Church above equally with the priesthood of the Church below, and the true union in divine worship of the Church below with the Church above, the true communion of Saints. So it falsely represents the Eucharistic offering as the offering of the Body and Blood of Christ on earth by the earthly priest alone for the Church, instead of the offering of the Body and Blood of Christ in Heaven by the Church on earth in union with the Church in Heaven, through the ministration only of the earthly priest. It represents the full consecration of the bread and wine to be the Body and Blood of Christ as effected by the mere utterance of the words of institution by the priest instead of by the prayers of the Church in and with that utterance, and by the invocation of the Holy Ghost in those prayers, and the divine answer to those prayers and invocation. It represents the Body and Blood of Christ as immediately "produced" on the earthly altar by the power of the individual priest as such, instead of as being made present or manifested in their heavenly sacrificial presence by the power of the Holy Ghost in answer to the earnest prayers and supplications of the whole Church.

And because Latin mediæval and later Roman sacerdotalism thus denies all true priesthood to the Church as such, it is not a true High-Churchism or a genuine legitimate development of the High-Church idea. High-Churchism, by its very name, implies the having a high idea of the Church as such. And the true High-Churchism, as the true sacerdotalism, is that which asserts the true priesthood of the Church as such, of which the priesthood of the individual priest as such is only a part and a certain subordinate function. The true sacerdotalism asserts this true priesthood of the Church to be no independent priesthood of the Church on earth, but a certain participation with the Church in Heaven in Christ's own exercise of His heavenly priesthood in the immediate presence of God, a participation which is effected in the power of the Holy Ghost by means of the whole worship of the public celebration of the Eucharist, the Church's faithful observance of Christ's Eucharistic institution.

This priesthood of the Church does not exclude, but includes the priesthood of the individual priest. The individual priest, because he is the minister of Christ, is also the minister of the Church, which is the Bride of Christ. He is therefore not the minister of Christ over His Church, but the minister of Christ to and with His Church. He does not minister *for* the Church as if *instead of* the Church, but *for* the Church as *with* the Church. He is the minister of God the Holy Ghost, because he has received the Holy Ghost for the office and work of a priest in the Church of God, committed to him by imposition of hands, but he is not the minister of the Holy Ghost as in him individually apart from the Church, but only of the Holy Ghost as the Holy Ghost is in and with the Church. The Pentecostal gift is in no one individually, except as the individual is in and with the whole Church.

A true sacerdotalism, then, though it does mean a priesthood of the Church as such above the priesthood of the individual priest, does not mean a priesthood of the laity as opposed to the priesthood of the clergy. The priesthood of the clergy is only for the sake of the manifestation and exercise of the priesthood of the laity, and the priesthood of the Church is that which includes the priesthood of both clergy and laity. Those who assert a universal priesthood of the laity as such apart from any special order of clergy are as far astray as those who assert an exclusive priesthood of the clergy. They only attribute to the laity a purely nominal priesthood, which is, in fact, to abolish all priesthood.

It is not enough then, to declaim against a false sacerdotalism, or to assert the falsehood of mediæval and Roman sacerdotalism. We must endeavour to assert, both by word and deed, the true sacerdotalism, the true priesthood of the whole Church, both clergy and laity, in the offering together of the Eucharistic sacrifice in order to our common participation with the Church in Heaven in Christ's own heavenly offering of His heavenly sacrifice. If Christ has made us all priests to God, He has only done so as He Himself is Priest to God, in the perpetual offering of His sacrifice, and as He enables us to take part in this perpetual offering by our offering together both priests and people the Eucharistic service of His appointment. And to assert this true sacerdotalism, the true priesthood of the whole Church in the offering together of the heavenly sacrifice of Christ in and by means of the Eucharistic service, is truly primitive and Catholic, which the more declaiming against mediæval sacerdotalism is not.

Next, as to the question of evangelicalism. There is a false evangelicalism, an evangelicalism falsely so-called, as well as a true sacerdotalism, the sacerdotalism which is essential to the very existence of the Church as the Body of Christ. It may reasonably be questioned whether any one of the multitudinous forms and shifting phases of ordinary English Protestantism, or all of them together, have the least right or title, historical or spiritual, to the epithet "evangelical;" their right to dub themselves "evangelical," with their Pharisaic assumption that Catholicism and sacerdotalism alone are essentially "unevangelical," may legitimately be challenged. Historically, and also so far spiritually, Lutheranism, that is the original Lutheranism of Luther himself and his immediate associates, has the best title to the epithet "evangelical;" it is the true evangelical Protestantism of the Reformation. Lutheranism, in its inception, was a truly evangelical protest against the unevangelical character of the later mediæval doctrine and practice of the Latin Church.

Without committing ourselves to all the extravagances of Luther's own expression of the doctrine or of later Lutheranism, we may yet agree that "justification by faith only" has a very true sense and a very real importance, as it was preached anew by Luther, and in opposition to a false doctrine and practice of justification by penances and indulgences, or of the deliverance of souls from purgatory by the priest's offering of Mass. But to Luther, and in original Lutheranism, "faith only" meant or included a great deal more than it was afterwards taken to mean in Calvinism or Zwinglianism, or by English Puritans and Methodists.

In original Lutheranism, justifying faith, however subjective in itself, was yet conceived as resting on the objective word of God, and not simply on that objective word as it is the dead letter of Scripture, but as it is the living word of Christ Himself, still uttered in the sacraments of Christ's own institution. Lutheran justifying faith thus meant, or included, faith in the living sacramental word of Christ, faith therefore in the grace of Baptism, faith in the real presence of Christ's Body and Blood in Holy Communion, faith in the real communion of that Body and Blood as really present, faith generally in the forgiveness of sins through Christ, the great privilege of the Gospel, as it is both signified and sealed by the sacraments of the Gospel. It has, therefore, every right to claim to be regarded as a truly "evangelic" faith, because it is a faith in Christ's own living preaching of the Gospel in the sacraments. The case is otherwise with faith in the Calvinist Zwinglian sense, or in the various senses in which it has been understood by English Puritans and Methodists.

In these later forms of Protestantism, justifying faith has been conceived, not merely as subjective in itself, but as resting on an altogether subjective foundation, on a subjective persuasion in a man's own mind or in some supposed presence or immediate inspiration of the Spirit of God, altogether independent of any use of sacraments. At the same time those who have thus insisted on the purely subjective character of justifying faith have also insisted on the necessity of faith in the objective word of God, conceived as the dead letter of Holy Scripture. They have thus created a certain dualism in Christian Faith, insisting on a purely subjective faith which alone is justifying, and an objective faith which, though not itself justifying, is yet necessary. In fact, it was speedily found out in the course of the Reformation movement, that the only way to prevent the purely subjective justifying faith from evaporating into fanatical delusion was to tie it artificially to an objective faith in the truth of God's written word in Holy Scripture. But just because there is this purely artificial connection between the two, there has always been the tendency in the subjective faith of Protestantism to part company with the objective.

But while Calvinist and Zwinglian Protestantism has thus somewhat inconsistently insisted on the importance and necessity of an objective faith in the written word, the mere dead letter of Holy Scripture, it has still more inconsistently represented this faith in the written word as absolutely excluding faith in the living spiritual power of the sacramental words of Christ even as they are delivered to us in that written word. Yet surely faith in the living spiritual power of the words of Christ as they are still uttered to us from Him in the sacraments of His appointment must be of far more importance to us than any faith in the mere dead letter of Holy Scripture. "The words that I speak unto you," Christ says, "they are spirit and they are life," and if Christ speaks His own words to us directly anywhere, it is surely in the Sacraments of His own appointment.

Yet a perverse Protestantism, which has so long pedantically insisted on the plenary inspiration and literal accuracy of every word of the written word, the mere dead letter of Holy Scripture, has had no scruple in denying the living spiritual power of the sacramental words of Christ; it has needlessly maintained the literal accuracy of everything in Scripture, but that of those solemn words of Christ, of which it is far more important for us to maintain the literal accuracy than of anything else in the whole world, such words as "Except a man be born of water and of the Spirit he cannot enter into the Kingdom of God;" "Except ye eat the flesh of the Son of Man, and drink His Blood, ye have no life in you;" "This is My Body which is given for you;" "This is My Blood which is shed for you." Under the guidance of its own prophets and Illuminati, it has resorted to all possible shifts and evasions of a merely human learning and human reasoning, in order to dispute the literal accuracy of these words of the Divine Truth, and explain away their real force and meaning for us.

The question, however, is not whether Protestantism is justified in so treating the words of Christ, but whether either its subjective justifying faith, which denies the real power and grace of the sacraments, or its faith in the written word, which denies the literal accuracy of the sacramental words, is a truly "evangelical" faith, a faith in the whole "pure" Gospel of Christ even as it is delivered to us in the written word. If the "pure" Gospel of Christ is contained for us anywhere, it is contained in the sacramental words of Christ. These words are Christ's own living declaration or preaching of His Gospel to us, His own application of that Gospel, His signature to His bestowal by means of them of all the precious gifts of His Gospel. They both declare to us what those gifts of the Gospel are, and are the means of giving them to us according to our capacity of receiving them, or as we put no hindrance in the way of our reception of them.

Baptismal regeneration is not sufficiently described as "a new birth into conditions of spiritual influence." It is better described in the words of our Lord Himself as a birth of the Spirit, which is a gift of the Spirit, by which a real entrance into the Kingdom of Heaven is ministered to us. It is a real gift of the Holy Spirit, which is, at the same time, the gift of the forgiveness of sins, the gift therefore of a new life and all the powers of a new life.

Holy Communion is the real communion of the real Body and Blood of Christ in that heavenly spiritual mode of existence in which they are also really present in the first instance with the Eucharistic bread and wine. If we are to say that "the Body of Christ is given, taken, and eaten in the Supper, only after an heavenly and spiritual manner," we are not so to take this as if it entitled us to contradict the other statement that "the Body and Blood of Christ are verily and indeed taken and received by the faithful in the Lord's Supper."

Without any real disloyalty to the Anglican Communion, we may indeed doubt whether the statement in the Article sufficiently comes up to the statement in Scripture, our Lord's own statement, and whether it is not susceptible of an interpretation which practically contradicts the statement of the Gospel.

Those who assert the Scriptures to be the supreme rule of faith must not assume the right to narrow down to their own theories the plain words of Scripture. Though the Body and Blood of Christ, being heavenly and spiritual, can only be eaten and drunk after an heavenly and spiritual manner, yet are they given and taken with the bread and wine, and not apart from them. And when it is further said, "the mean whereby the Body of Christ is received and eaten in the Supper is faith," we are not justified in understanding that subjective faith creates for itself that spiritual presence, or that faith alone, and not love, is the means whereby the Body of Christ is truly partaken of to our spiritual nourishment. Here, if anywhere, faith must work by love, and it is love, the heavenly love kindled and shed abroad in our hearts by God the Holy Ghost, that truly eats and drinks the Body and Blood of Christ, as they are Eucharistically given by the heavenly love of Christ Himself.

To say that mere faith so-called in the Atonement of Christ is the eating and drinking of the Body and Blood of Christ, whether in the Sacrament or out of it, is to presume to be wiser than the Master Himself, Who has given His Body and Blood to be eaten and drunk by means of their presence, in the first instance, with the Eucharistic bread and wine. The gifts of Christ in His Sacraments then are the true gifts of the Gospel, and there can be no true faith in the Gospel which in any way denies, or depreciates, or makes superfluous the grace of the Sacraments, that is, the living spiritual truth and power of Christ's own words as intended by Christ Himself to be objectively realized for us in His Sacraments by reason of His very appointment of those Sacraments. The actual Sacraments ministered to us in His Church are a real part of that truth of the Gospel in which we have to believe, because as being Christ's own appointed application of His Gospel, they are the guarantee to us of the living spiritual truth and power of His words as recorded in the Gospel. We cannot truly believe in the living spiritual truth and power of Christ's words in the written Gospel unless we also believe in the realization of that truth and power for us in the Sacraments.

The true Scriptural evangelicalism, therefore, can only be that which admits the literal, that is, the living spiritual, truth of Christ's own words to be realized for us in and by means of the Sacraments, and which does not presume to claim the spiritual gifts of Christ's Gospel otherwise than on the ground of the Sacraments of the Gospel.

With what right, then, can the ordinary Calvinist Zwinglian Protestantism, prevalent in England and elsewhere, dub itself either Scriptural or evangelical, which takes upon itself to deny the literal truth of Christ's own words in the Gospel with reference to the Sacraments, and on the ground of its own peculiar theory of faith denies or depreciates, or make superfluous the reality of sacramental grace, the reality of sacramental presence? The original Lutheranism of the Reformation had indeed a right to regard itself as so far truly Scriptural and Evangelical, not only because of its protest against unscriptural and unevangelical doctrines and practices of the Church of Rome, but because of its own positive belief in the reality of sacramental grace and the literal truth of our Lord's sacramental words. If Luther preached justifying faith, it was a justifying faith not divorced from faith in the Sacraments, but professing only to be derived from, and continually basing itself upon, faith in the Word of Christ living in the Sacraments. It was a faith which had to be founded upon the reality of baptismal grace, and to be sustained by the reality of the Eucharistic presence.

And thus to Luther, faith in the Divine Word was not simply faith in the written word of Scripture, the mere dead letter, but faith in the living word of Christ as objectively and also to be subjectively realized in His Sacraments. Luther was only not evangelical enough by unduly limiting sacramental grace itself to justifying faith, and so, in effect, denying the objective fulness of the grace of God in Christ, that fulness of all the blessings of the Gospel as communicated by Sacraments, which is summed up in the scriptural expression, "the participation of the Divine Nature, the fulness of God Himself." (2 Peter i. 4; Eph. iii. 19.)

However this may be, Lutheran Protestantism was truly evangelical in a sense in which the later Calvinistic Zwinglian Protestantism is not, because it recognized the word of Christ in the Gospel as living for us in the Sacraments. The justifying faith of later Protestantism has denied the living character of the word of Christ in Sacraments, has claimed to be independent of the reality of baptismal grace and of the reality of the Eucharistic presence, and though professing to be derived from the written word, has practically dispensed with all other foundation and support but its own proud consciousness of itself. But in denying the living character of the word of Christ in Sacraments, it not only degrades the word of Christ, but is contrary to that written word which delivers to us the word of Christ.

In so degrading the word of Christ, it is profoundly unevangelical, as in this contrariety to the written word it is distinctly unscriptural. Yet with the clear witness of original Lutheranism against it, this unscriptural and unevangelical Zwinglian Calvinism has had the effrontery not only to dub itself alone scriptural and evangelical even in its denial and rejection of the living spiritual truth of Christ's own words, but to characterize the Catholic faith in that living spiritual truth as it has been held by ordinary English High Churchmen as "unscriptural," "unevangelical," and even as "gross superstition."

Granting that there has been reason to complain of Roman and mediæval doctrine as "unscriptural," "unevangelical" by excess, that is, by addition of unscriptural, unevangelical elements to the Scriptural evangelical doctrine of a primitive Catholicism, there is equal reason to complain of ordinary Protestant doctrine as "unscriptural" and "unevangelical" by defect, and that the serious defect of the rejection of Christ's own words in the Gospel in their plain meaning, only for the sake of its own pet theory of the sole or supreme importance of subjective faith. Protestantism indeed must first take heed to cast out the beam of its own unscriptural, unevangelical defects, before it can ever see clearly to cast out the mote of the Roman unscriptural and unevangelical excesses of doctrine or practice.

Is a true evangelicalism inconsistent with a true sacerdotalism? Undoubtedly it is with the false sacerdotalism which magnifies the priesthood of the individual priest above the true priesthood of the whole Church of Christ, and even above the heavenly priesthood of Christ Himself, but not with the true sacerdotalism which subordinates the priesthood of the individual priest in the Church to the priesthood of the whole Body of Christ, and again, the priesthood of the whole Body of Christ to the heavenly priesthood of Christ Himself.

It has been admitted above that original Lutheranism has the best right to the title of "Protestant Evangelicalism." It has however been hinted, at the same time, that though evangelical in its principle, it was not evangelical enough. It unduly limited the blessings of the Gospel by reducing them all to the one blessing of "justifying faith;" it practically denied the objective fulness of the grace of God in Christ, and communicated to us by Sacraments; it emphasized the purely passive receptive attitude of Christian faith towards the grace of Christ, but ignored that higher privilege of active co-operation with Himself to which Christ by that very grace calls His Church.

And so, though it is Lutheranism that has in the first instance created the tradition that evangelicalism as such is opposed to all sacerdotalism so-called and to all doctrine of a Eucharistic sacrifice, yet in this latter respect more especially, not only was Lutheranism not evangelical enough, but in spite of, and yet also by the very nature of its opposition to the Roman doctrine of the sacrifice of the Mass, it has only cleared the ground for the assertion of a truer doctrine of the sacrifice of the Eucharist, the assertion of a true offering of the Body and Blood of Christ in the Eucharist.

Luther and original Lutheranism indeed may be said to have laid down right principles on many points of controversial theology, but not always to have drawn the right conclusions. A later Protestantism greedily welcomed the negative conclusions of Luther, but rejected, without much scruple, either the positive conclusions or the positive principles on which alone he professed to found his negative conclusions. So even in the question of "justifying faith," while Luther derived and deduced his doctrine from his faith in the living word of Christ in the Sacraments, the later Protestantism adopted his conclusion only to deny his premises; it used the doctrine of justifying faith in order to reject and deny the grace and power of the Sacraments, substituting for the true premises of Luther false premises of its own, faith in the written word only, or faith in immediate inspiration without Sacraments. So again in the question of the Eucharist, while Luther denied the sacrifice on the very ground of the real presence, later Protestantism assumed his denial of the sacrifice only for the sake of impugning even his doctrine of the real presence.

Romanism indeed has greatly profited by this unfortunate tendency in mere Protestantism to proceed to further and further negative conclusions. False negative conclusions only give a greater appearance of weight and authority to the false positive doctrines opposed to them. There is this double danger that continually besets all purely negative conclusions, both to be false themselves by reason of their purely negative character, and to give greater appearance of weight and authority to even more false positive doctrines. Luther was right in denying the Roman doctrine of the sacrifice of the Mass, but wrong in not substituting, or attempting to substitute, a truer doctrine of the sacrifice in its place. He was right in denying the Roman sacrifice of the Mass on the ground of the evangelical doctrine of the real presence, but other Protestants are altogether out of court who base their denial of the sacrifice on their denial of the real presence. The doctrine of the real presence is a Catholic evangelical doctrine, and no doctrine can be primitive or Catholic or evangelical which denies it. It is a Catholic doctrine only because it is an evangelical doctrine, a doctrine of the Gospel of Christ, which from the first has been received as such by the Catholic Church of Christ throughout the world. Does it require proof that it is a doctrine of the Gospel of Christ? It is so, because and so far as it is the simple acceptance of Christ's own declaration in the Gospel, "This is My Body," "This is My Blood," which is at the same time the acceptance of Christ's own preaching of the Gospel, the Gospel of the Atoning Sacrifice of His Cross and Passion, for Christ not only said, "This is My Body," "This is My Blood," but "This is My Body which is given for you," "This is

My Blood which is shed for you and for many for the remission of sins," "The cup of the New Testament in My Blood." And these words of Christ are His message or His preaching of the Gospel to us, not simply as they are words of His historically delivered to us in the written Gospel, but as they are by His appointment and command delivered to us in the actual living Gospel of the Eucharistic celebration, as the written Gospel itself testifies, "Do this in remembrance of Me."

Can it be "evangelical" to reject or fritter away the plain meaning of our Lord's own words, which are at the same time His own real preaching of His Gospel to us? The Gospel of the Atonement, as it is still preached to us from Christ Himself and by His command, must rest on the Gospel of the Eucharistic Presence. We only know from Christ Himself that His Body was given for us upon the Cross, His Blood shed for the forgiveness of our sins, from the words by which He instituted His Sacrament, and which by His own appointment He still speaks to us in every proper celebration of His Sacrament, as He speaks them to us nowhere else and in no other way. But He can only be understood to speak to us this message of His Gospel in the Eucharistic celebration as He also speaks to us the truth of His real presence. He only Himself assures us of the truth of His Atonement as He assures us of the truth of His sacramental presence.

From a true evangelical point of view, then, Luther was fully justified in refusing to surrender the doctrine of the real presence, or to accept any interpretation of the words of Christ in the Eucharistic institution which did violence to the reality of their meaning. He was right in regarding the doctrine of the real presence to be as real and essential a part of the Gospel of Christ as the doctrine of the Atonement, because it is Christ's own assurance to us of the truth of His Atonement. Luther was only not evangelical enough by thus limiting the significance of the real presence to the mere assurance of the Atonement; he did not himself do full justice to the Eucharistic words. He so far disconnected the one half of the Eucharistic words from the other half, and while he passionately contended for the literal meaning of the words, "This is My Body," "This is My Blood," he ignored the full literal meaning of the words in their whole connection, "This is My Body given for you," "My Blood shed for you." So while he regarded the latter half of the words as Christ's own message of the Gospel, he did not regard the whole words as Christ's very gift of the Gospel, the gift of His Atonement, and the gift of His Atonement only, as being the gift of the Atoning Sacrifice itself. So, too, while he regarded the Eucharist as the real presence and communion of Christ's Body and Blood, as a means of assurance of the Atonement wrought upon the Cross, he did not rise to its full evangelical significance as the real presence and communion of the Atoning Sacrifice itself as it continues to be offered for us by Christ Himself before God in Heaven.

Luther, however, is not to be blamed for not at once rising to the perception of this fuller evangelical significance of the Eucharistic presence; he was hampered by an imperfect theory of the Atonement, held by him in common with Romanists and other Protestants, inherited from mediæval times, a theory which denies the continued offering in Heaven of the atoning sacrifice in the attained fulness of its atoning power. On the ground, however, of that evangelical doctrine of the real presence which he did hold, and so far as it went, he was right in denying both the Roman doctrines of Transubstantiation and the sacrifice of the Mass. The real presence could only be a real presence of Christ's Body and Blood, as it was the presence of Christ's glorified Body and Blood, a presence which, because it is a heavenly glorified presence, needs not to effect any destruction or cessation, still less any conversion or absorption, of the mere so-called substances of the earthly bread and wine with which it is associated.

And even if Christ's Body and Blood as thus present were capable of being offered by men upon earth, as Romanists allege, yet is this offering of them no "true and proper" sacrifice of them, nor is it capable of being accepted as such by God in Heaven. The sacrifice of the Cross as offered on Calvary is the only "true and proper" sacrifice of the Body and Blood of Christ, the only propitiatory offered of them. And certainly from the point of view, common to both Lutherans and Romanists, of the denial of any continued offering of the sacrifice of the Cross, this argument is irrefragable.

So also the further argument, the presence as thus given is given for communion only, not for offering. It is undoubtedly true that if the Body and Blood of Christ are not given with the bread and wine as they are or have been offered, they are not given to be offered. But what if they are given only as they are being continually offered? Granting all that may be urged against the Roman assertion of a new offering or a new mode of offering in the Mass of the Body and Blood of Christ as a "true and proper" sacrifice, it all avails nothing against the assertion of the continued offering of the sacrifice of the Cross by Christ Himself in Heaven.

The Lutheran assertions and arguments only clear the way for the assertion of the true doctrine of the Eucharistic sacrifice. The Lutheran assertion of the doctrine of the real presence on the ground of the simple evangelical acceptance of the Eucharistic words of Christ is the very basis of the true doctrine. The Lutherans themselves were only not faithful enough to their evangelical principle by not taking these words in the full extent of their evangelical meaning.

The evangelical gift in the Holy Eucharist is not of the mere Body and Blood of Christ to be received as an assurance of the Atonement of the Cross, but as the words of Christ themselves plainly testify, it is the gift of the very Body and Blood of the Atoning Sacrifice, the gift of the sacrifice itself, as it continues to be offered before God in Heaven in order to be so given to men.

It is not right, and still less is it evangelical, to interpret the words of Christ in the Eucharistic institution by our own preconceived theories of Atonement and of the nature of the Atoning Sacrifice. On the contrary, if we are to be truly evangelical, we must base all our theories of the Atonement and of the nature of the Atoning Sacrifice on

Christ's own words which expressly declare that Sacrifice and Atonement. In face of our Lord's own words, what right have we to say that the Atoning Sacrifice ceased to be offered with the death of Calvary? It was only then that the atoning power of the sacrifice began to be developed, first by the descent into hell, then the resurrection from the dead, and then by the ascension into Heaven.

And how is it consistent with the typical sacrifices of the Old Testament to regard the Atonement as effected or the sacrifice as fully offered by the mere death of the victim, and not rather by the sprinkling of the sacrificial blood after death, and the acceptance and divine transfiguration of the victim by the sacrificial flames of the altar-fire? And how is all this fulfilled in Christ but by the resurrection and ascension and the continued offering in Heaven, Christ's entrance into the holiest with and through His own precious Blood, that is, with and through His own complete sacrifice. His sacrifice of the Cross does not merely consist in the surrender of His life to death, but in the offering of His death as the means of giving us life. Not in His death itself therefore does He offer or fully offer the sacrifice of His death, but only in His risen and ascended life. And His risen and ascended life itself is part of the Atoning Sacrifice as He now offers it for us, for it is the fruit of His death, the reward of His obedience unto death, the token of the divine acceptance of the sacrifice, without which it would not be an atoning propitiatory sacrifice.

Modern Lutheran theologians, as Kurtz and others, have recognized the symbolic and typical importance of the blood-sprinkling in connection with the sacrifices of the Old Dispensation, and have thence inferred that the sacrifice of Calvary is not fully offered until the ascension into Heaven, but that, as then for the first time completely offered, it afterwards ceases to be offered. The former part of this inference is correct, but not the latter. It is as great a mistake to say that the sacrifice ceases to be offered with the ascension as with the death on Calvary. The perfect sacrifice does not cease to be offered, even when it is completely offered. Rather, it continues to be offered, and in the continuance of the offering consists the perpetual exercise of Christ's heavenly priesthood, the priesthood for ever after the order of Melchizedek. Christ, as Man, "appears in the presence of God for us," to be our High-Priestly Advocate and Intercessor, no otherwise than in this perpetual offering of the one perfect Atoning Sacrifice, which He continues to offer in the power of the same Eternal Spirit of Divine holiness and love through Whom He began the offering of it upon earth. And it is in the power of this perpetual offering in Heaven that, by means of the Eucharistic service He has appointed for His Church on earth, He gives His Body and Blood, no otherwise His Body and Blood than as they are the Body and Blood of the Atoning Sacrifice which He continues to offer in Heaven, the sacrifice of the Cross. The real presence and communion are not of the Body and Blood merely, as Luther said, but of the Body and Blood of the Atoning Sacrifice of the Cross as it continues to be offered by Christ in Heaven, for so only is communion a true participation of the sacrifice. Unless the sacrifice continued to be offered, communion would be no true participation of the sacrifice, and communion is absolutely valueless except as it is the participation of the heavenly sacrifice.

So are all offerings fulfilled in the sacrifice of Christ—the burnt-offering, the sin-offering, the peace-offering, and Christ has willed the continuance of His sacrificial offering, that He may grant to His people the true participation of His sacrifice. So is His priesthood in Heaven truly described as a priesthood for ever after the order of Melchizedek, because he brings forth from the heavenly sanctuary, where He continues to offer, the Body and Blood of the Atoning Sacrifice, which He offers to be to His people the true bread and wine, the bread and wine of eternal life. So indeed with the bread and wine of the Church's own Eucharistic offering He gives His Body and Blood, as offered by Himself in Heaven, not in order to be offered by means of the bread and wine in any new offering of them on earth distinct from the offering in Heaven.

But this is not all, there is more than this mere passive reception of the sacrifice of Christ. Because His sacrifice still lives in Heaven in His own perpetual offering of it, Christ calls His Church by means of the Eucharistic celebration, not only to the participation of that sacrifice in Holy Communion, but to take part with Him in the perpetual offering of it. And the Church is only able to partake of the sacrifice offered, as she first takes part with Christ in the heavenly offering, and therefore by the preparatory sprinkling of His precious Blood in Holy Baptism to obedience and sanctification of the

Spirit, has He enabled His Church by her own obedient Eucharistic offering of bread and wine, to "draw near with a true heart in full assurance of faith," and to have "boldness to enter into the holiest," that is, into the immediate presence of God, where He continues to offer for us the Atoning Sacrifice, "by the new and living way which He hath consecrated for us through the veil of His flesh," the new and living way of His risen and ascended life, "to enter into the holiest" in the power of that Spirit which He sends forth upon us to enable us so to do, and to take part with Him in His never-ceasing work of intercession and propitiation for us and the whole world in the offering of His sacrifice, for His work is only a work of intercession, as it is also a work of propitiation. He is only our "Advocate with the Father," as He is still the "propitiation for our sins." (1 John ii. 1, 2.) And therefore also is it a grievous sin, as the writer of the Epistle to the Hebrews so strongly insists, to "forsake the assembling of ourselves together" in the Church's Eucharistic celebration, for it is to "tread under foot the Son of God, and to count the blood of the covenant wherewith we have been sanctified an unholy thing, and to do despite to the Spirit of grace." This is the true Atonement which Christ has provided for us by His Atoning Sacrifice, this power of presenting ourselves before God with purified hearts and consciences with the whole Church of God in earth and Heaven, so as to take part in the true worship of God by Christ, the "High Priest over the house of God," the true worship of Christ Himself our heavenly King.

In this doctrine of the Eucharistic presence and the heavenly sacrifice, founded as it is on the strictest evangelical interpretation of Christ's own words in the Eucharistic institution, and on the plain teaching of the Epistle to the Hebrews, a true evangelicalism is shewn to be one with a true sacerdotalism. As little as it is a true sacerdotalism, which maintains that Christ only now exercises His office of priesthood through the ministers of His Church on earth, as little is it a true Scriptural evangelicalism, which denies the living power and heavenly existence of the sacrifice of Christ, and that evangelical privilege which Christ has bestowed upon His Church on earth of taking part with Him in the heavenly offering of His sacrifice, and so uniting her worship of God with the worship of God by the Church Triumphant in Heaven.

With other points raised by Archdeacon Sinclair in his pamphlet there is no occasion here to deal. It is sufficient to have pointed out that to adopt a mere negative attitude towards so-called sacerdotalism is an entire mistake, and however this opposition to all sacerdotalism may have become part of the Protestant evangelical tradition of the last three hundred and fifty years, it is not in accordance with the "primitive Catholic" evangelicalism of the Gospel itself, or of the teaching of the Apostles as represented by the Epistle to the Hebrews and the writings of S. John. If Protestant evangelicals "altogether distrust tradition," let them also distrust their own tradition so far as it is not in accordance with or does not come up to the full evangelical tradition in the New Testament itself.

www.ingramcontent.com/pod-product-compliance
Lightning Source LLC
Chambersburg PA
CBHW030307170426
43202CB00009B/904